FORMS OF
ROMAN LEGISLATION

Oxford University Press, Amen House, London E.C. 4

GLASGOW NEW YORK TORONTO MELBOURNE WELLINGTON
BOMBAY CALCUTTA MADRAS KARACHI CAPE TOWN IBADAN

Geoffrey Cumberlege, Publisher to the University

FORMS OF
ROMAN LEGISLATION

BY

DAVID DAUBE

OXFORD
AT THE CLARENDON PRESS
1956

PRINTED IN GREAT BRITAIN

TO

HUGH LAST

PREFACE

THIS volume grew out of lectures delivered at University College, London, with the late Professor H. F. Jolowicz in the Chair, and at the University of Aberdeen, with Principal T. M. Taylor in the Chair. I am indebted for criticism and encouragement to Professor P. W. Duff of Cambridge University, and Professor A. Cameron and Mr. P. G. Stein of Aberdeen University.

D. D.

CONTENTS

I

II

I

1. Introduction

CONSIDERING how much attention has been devoted to great
and small things in Roman law, it is surprising to find questions
of legislative form almost completely neglected. A story of
Gellius comes to mind. He tells us how one day he came across
a difficult legal term in an ancient epic. So he asked a professor
of literature what it meant. But he also did not know, and
advised Gellius in these words: 'I would have you believe me
when I say that Quintus Ennius learned this, not from a study
of poetry, but from someone skilled in the law. Do you too,
then, go and learn from the same source as Ennius.' Modern
writers on Roman law seem to take the view that the authors
of the XII Tables and their successors must have learned about
form or style, not from someone skilled in the law, but from a
study of poetry; and they would fain send us to the professor
of literature for information on matters of this kind. But the
time has surely come for a more positive approach.

Up to some thirty years ago the history of ancient literature
was dominated by source criticism. The principal question in
dealing with an ancient author was: Does he draw on any
previous authors, and if so, what are their respective shares?
Thus the experts on Homer were chiefly interested in the composition of the epic, i.e. the various parts from which it is
constructed and the relation between them. For example, in
Book IX of the Iliad, Agamemnon offers Achilles princely atone-
ment. In XVI, Achilles complains that Agamemnon will make
no amends. The two passages, the source critics pointed out,
must originally have belonged to different versions; some com-
piler brought them together, despite the contradiction that
ensued.

The results reached by generations of scholars who analysed

5876   B

the material in this manner have lost nothing of their importance. The division of the Pentateuch into two mainly narrative
sources, the Yahvist and the Elohist, and two mainly legislative
ones, Deuteronomy and the Priestly Code, in whatever form
we accept it, and even if we do not accept it, still furnishes a
useful basis for further investigation. Similarly, we shall not
lightly discard the view, worked out in the course of the last
century, that both Matthew and Luke used the gospel of Mark.
In the field of Roman law, a great deal of work has been done
about the commentaries on Sabinus, portions of which are
preserved in the Digest, with a view to finding out how much
may be ascribed to Sabinus, and how much to the commen-
tators or even later revisers.[1]

However, in the past few decades a new method has been
developed by which it is hoped to penetrate farther into the
origins of ancient works than mere source criticism can take
us. The principal question no longer is: What authors can we
distinguish? It is: What formal units can we distinguish? And
the aim is to break through to forms prior to any definite
source, and thereby to discover the factors ultimately respon-
sible for the growth and preservation of an idea. This method is
called form criticism.

It proceeds from two observations. First, in an early age,
and especially so long as transmission takes place by word of
mouth, the various literary forms are products not so much of
the artistic whim of this or that poet as of communal experience
and communal needs. Hymns, war-cries, riddles, legends and
so forth have each their fixed, peculiar style adapted to a
definite, practical requirement of society: they each have their
'setting in life'. There is far less arbitrary, unnecessary devia-
tion from pattern than in modern, written, individualistic
literature.

Secondly, the form of a piece of literature often remains
unchanged even when that piece is incorporated in a larger
work of an entirely different nature. For example, in an epistle
of Paul the form will still betray the origin of one section in

[1] By far the most important specimen is still *Das Sabinussystem* by Lenel, 1892.

catechetical teaching, of another in academic exegesis of Scripture, of a third in liturgy; and the form will do this even though in all these sections we may be told exactly the same thing as far as substance is concerned—say, that humiliation means exaltation.

Once these two observations are admitted, viz. that early forms are expressions of communal needs and that they tend to survive transplanting to alien soil, it follows that we must concentrate on form if we are to arrive at the ultimate social data underlying any material before us. Source criticism is indispensable for establishing the authorship of a work or its several parts. Beyond that, for discovering the original function of an idea, its setting in life, form criticism is the method to employ.

There are, indeed, cases where an understanding of form will lead to the detection of errors committed by source criticism; as when an abrupt change in metre or the like, which had been imputed to the intervention of a second author, can be accounted for by the specific needs prevailing in a branch of communal activity. In Matthew,[1] whereas the first eight beatitudes are of the type 'Blessed are the poor', the last introduces the second person, 'Blessed are ye'; it is also longer and more comprehensive. (Luke,[2] who puts 'Blessed are ye' throughout, is smoother but no doubt secondary.) Yet the last beatitude should not, on this account, be considered an addition. The pattern can be paralleled from ancient Jewish liturgy—first a number of fairly short lines with the quiet third person, then an outpouring in the ardent direct address. That this form has a real function to fulfil, both in worship and sermon, will hardly be doubted.

In this lecture I wish to suggest that form criticism may be profitably applied to problems of legal history; and more particularly, that it may help us to a deeper insight into the background of Roman legislation.

[1] 5. 3 ff. See Daube, *Journal of Theological Studies* 45, 1944, 21 ff.
[2] 6. 20 ff.

2. Four Questions

To mention only four points, never noticed, still less explained, yet surely remarkable enough—and quite elementary. When putting a case, a lawgiver may use a conditional clause, 'If', or a relative clause, 'He who' or 'Whoever'. He may say 'If a man murders another man, he shall be put to death' or 'Whoever murders a man shall be put to death'. In early Roman legislation, the latter type is extremely rare; by the close of the Republic, it is just as frequent as the former. The *lex Aquilia*, an old statute, runs: 'If anyone kills another's slave—or, If anyone inflicts loss on another by wounding his slave—he shall be bound to pay.'[1] A law enacted under Augustus runs: 'Whoever damages a water-channel shall be bound to pay.'[2] What is there behind this change?

Or take this question. In Latin the place of an imperative or jussive is often taken by phrases like 'it is needful to do this or that', *oportet*, *necesse est*. But the form hardly ever occurs in legislation. Why not? Why do we hardly ever find 'If anyone damages another's property, it will be needful for him to pay', instead of the imperative, 'he shall be bound to pay', *damnas esto?* Again, why do we nevertheless find it here and there? A statute ascribed to Numa ordains: 'If a man is killed by lightning, it is not proper to celebrate any funeral rites for him', *ei iusta nulla fieri oportet*.[3] And a list of rules to be observed by the priests of Jupiter—admittedly not legislation proper—contains seventeen or eighteen injunctions of the type *oportet*, 'it is needful', and not a single imperative or jussive.[4] The following nine expressions are used: *oportet, necessum est, mos est,*

[1] Bruns, *Fontes*, 7th ed. by Gradenwitz (on the basis of 6th ed. by Mommsen), 1909, 45 f.

[2] Bruns, 113.

[3] Bruns, 8. *Oportere* recurs in the statute by Numa quoted immediately after this one in Bruns.

[4] Gellius 10. 15. 1 ff. We obtain eighteen if we include the quotation from Varro, 10. 15. 32. As for an alleged jussive *detonset*, see below, pp. 71 f.

fas est, ius est, religio est, piaculum est, licitum est, constitutum est—
but never a 'they shall' or 'shall not'.

A third observation. A lawgiver who wishes to impose a
penalty on a wrongful act has the choice between either of
these forms. He may issue a command or prohibition, followed
by a sanction. The praetor's Edict says: 'Nothing may be done
on purpose to bring infamy on a man. If anyone acts contrary
to this, I shall go into the case.'[1] But it is also possible to announce order and sanction in one. In the same section of the
Edict, we find the provisions: 'Whoever publicly rails at a
man in an objectionable manner, against him I shall give an
action', and 'If anyone accosts or follows a matron in an
objectionable manner, I shall take steps.'[2] Here there are no
special decrees forbidding the misdeeds in question, public
insults and indecent addresses. The praetor immediately states
what will be the consequences if a certain offence is committed.
The prohibition of that offence is only implied. Both types, the
separate order followed by a separate sanction—'Do this; otherwise you will be punished'—and the order and sanction in
one—'If you do not do this, you will be punished'—are common from the earliest period of Roman law. When does a lawgiver use the one and when the other?

Again, the praetor and aediles promise an action now 'if so
and so has occurred', *quod (si) factum erit*, now 'if so and so is
alleged to have occurred', *quod (si) factum esse dicetur*. On the
one hand we find 'From whatever house anything has been
thrown down, I shall give an action against its occupant' or
'If expense has been incurred through a burial, I shall give an
action for its recovery'; on the other 'If a free man is alleged to
have perished', 'Whatever anyone is alleged to have lent'.[3]
The reference to allegation is alien to the style of statutes,
senatusconsults and jurists. Any exceptions are apparent rather
than real. Why is it typically edictal? Why do praetor and
aediles use the simpler form, 'if so and so has occurred', as
well? When do they use 'if so and so has occurred' and when
'if so and so is alleged to have occurred'?

[1] Lenel, *Edictum*, 3rd ed., 1927, 401.   [2] Lenel, 400.   [3] Lenel, 173, 229, 252.

It might be objected to this kind of approach that such differences signify nothing. If form criticism is right, however, this cannot be so. Oscar Wilde remarks that when a woman speaks to you, you should listen not to what she says, but to how she says it. In ancient times, that would have applied to men as well. If form criticism is right, not only must there be a serious explanation of the differences mentioned, but that explanation may well open vistas which remain closed so long as we concern ourselves solely with what a lawgiver says, but not with how he says it. Let us go through the four simple points I have raised and see what we can make of them.

A. Conditional Clause and Relative Clause

First, then, in early Roman legislation, the form 'If a man murders another man, he shall be put to death' predominates, whereas later, the form 'Whoever murders a man shall be put to death' is no less usual. This change reflects an evolution from what we might call folk-law to a legal system. 'If a man does this or that' tells you a story—though of something yet to come. It puts a situation which may arise, and informs you how to meet it. 'Whoever does this or that' refers, not to a situation, but to a category, a person defined by his action. It does not inform you how to meet a contingency, but declares the proper treatment of a murderer. It is more general, abstract, detached.

The different settings in life of the two forms of law become quite clear when we consider the different questions to which they make answer. The 'If'-form answers to the question: 'What shall be done in a certain emergency, if this or that happens, if a man murders another man?' Answer: 'In that emergency, if a man murders another man, he shall be put to death.' The relative clause presupposes a more advanced mode of asking: 'What shall be done to a certain class of persons, to him who murders?' Answer: 'That class, whoever murders a man, shall be put to death.' Here lies the reason why the old *lex Aquilia* begins, 'If anyone kills another's slave', but a statute from the time of Augustus, 'Whoever damages a water-channel'. The story has become a category.

This interpretation of the conditional form as less abstract than the relative is confirmed by a pronounced difference in their use, persisting at least until the end of the Principate. Where a lawgiver subdivides a case into several alternatives, he very frequently introduces the main case by a relative clause and the subordinate alternatives by 'If'-clauses; but we never once find the converse. There are scores of provisions in the statutes, senatusconsults and edicts like this one, of the praetor: 'Through whose-ever wickedness a tomb is interfered with, against him I shall give an action for 100,000 sesterces. If anyone makes his habitation in a tomb, against him I shall give an action for 200,000.'[1] But there is not a single regulation starting 'If anyone interferes with a tomb' and going on to open an exceptionally bad possibility with 'Whoever makes his habitation in a tomb'. To this extent, the conditional form and the relative form continue in their respective original roles, the one contemplating a particular emergency, the other of a systematic character.

We may note, in passing, that had adequate attention been paid to such questions of form, a misleading arrangement in Bruns could have been avoided. Bruns[2] prints an edict concerning mob violence in which, contrary to our result, the principal case appears in an 'If'-clause, followed by a rather more special case—where a wrong is done during a riot—in a relative clause: 'If loss has wickedly been inflicted on anyone through armed men, I shall give an action. Through whose-ever wickedness loss has been inflicted during a riot, against him I shall give an action.'

As a matter of fact, however, the two cases were not regulated at the same time at all; more than that, even Julian in his redaction did not combine them. The edict about armed men

---

[1] Lenel, 228. Fisher, Fraser and Ross, in *The Scottish Geographical Magazine* 69, no. 1, 1953, 27, say that watertanks which they discovered in an old burial ground in Cyrenaica must have been used for irrigation, since the burial ground 'was presumably uninhabited'. But they themselves found a tomb at present occupied by an Arab family; and that this kind of thing happened in antiquity is shown by the Roman decrees against it. It is not, therefore, *a priori* impossible that the tanks date from a time when the burial ground was converted into a settlement.

[2] 227.

figures prominently in Pro Tullio; that about a riot presumably also dates from the Republic, but it is first mentioned by Labeo. It is, indeed, far less intimately connected with that about armed men than with another edict first mentioned by Labeo, which deals with delicts committed in time of fire, shipwreck and so on. In Ulpian's commentary on Julian's redaction, the three edicts—about armed men, about a riot, and about fire &c.—are quoted as three distinct units, each introduced by *praetor ait* and the commentary on each opening with *hoc edictum* or the like. Lenel rightly gives them as three separate edicts.[1] The second case, then, is not subordinate to the first; it is an independent, fresh case.

A comparison with the use of conditional and relative clauses in other ancient systems of law would show that the thesis I am advancing is of universal application. Old Testament legislation furnishes a striking parallel. But I shall not here elaborate this aspect.

B. *'It is proper'*

My next point was that such substitutes for the imperative as *oportet, necesse est,* 'It is correct, needful', are most uncommon in legislation, though, at first sight at any rate, not quite absent. The explanation is that these phrases express, not a direct command—'I order you to do this or that'—and not even a freely formed opinion—'In my view you should do this or that' —but a reference to some higher authority—'There are compelling reasons for doing this or that.' If I tell a person that 'it is proper' or 'improper' to behave in a certain way, I am not deciding myself but am introducing a recognized standard, be it of morality, of religion, of social convention, or any other sphere. An independent lawgiver, therefore, will prefer a real imperative, 'This or that shall be done', implying 'I command it to be done', whereas the form 'It is proper to do this or that' comes well from a wise man who knows by what reasons your actions ought to be guided, who can tell you the right course to take in a difficulty. In other words, as far as legal usage is

[1] 391, 395 f.

concerned, the setting in life of this form, 'it is correct, needful', is not the making of law, but the understanding and interpreting of law. When Mr. Churchill gave orders, he said: 'You should board *Altmark*'[1] or 'Speak to me about this.'[2] But in the last days of 1939 he proposed to notify the C.-in-C., Mediterranean, that 'the three-mile limit only need be observed'.[3] Here he was stating his interpretation of our international obligations.

Etymology is not always a safe guide. But it is surely relevant that *oportet*—*ob-vortet*—primarily means 'it turns this way', 'the favourable direction is this way'; and an ancient exclamation like *di bene vortant* suggests that the direction is supplied by religion. We may compare the English adjective 'toward'— 'to-ward', the second part being related to *vertere*. At first it signifies 'destined to turn out', 'future', then 'apt' and so on; while 'untoward' signifies 'ill-adapted', 'unlucky'.

Once we have grasped the function of 'it is correct, needful', we are in a position to appreciate the few statutes where such a phrase does appear instead of an imperative. They belong without exception to the sacred law. 'If a man is killed by lightning, *ei iusta nulla fieri oportet*, it is not permissible to celebrate the funeral rites for him': evidently, this is not the decree of a free lawgiver, a lawgiver who might, if he liked, enjoin the opposite. It is, essentially, interpretation; it is the wise men's reading of the divine will. The priests (unless they speak as prophets, as the direct messengers of a god, or, indeed, usurp the forms of secular authority) do not dictate to you. They inform you of the results of their studies of sacred things.

It may, indeed, be questioned whether any of these directions with *oportet* were statutes, *leges*, in the strict sense at all— though to be sure they are classed as such in the sources—and even whether they were edicts of magistrates.[4] They look much more like pontifical pronouncements. Be this as it may, it is this fact, that sacred affairs must be conducted in accordance, not with any arbitrary decisions, but with the *oportere*, with

[1] Gathering Storm, 1948, 444.   [2] 601.   [3] 593.
[4] See Mommsen, *Staatsrecht*, vol. ii, pt. 1, 3rd ed., 1887, 41 ff. As for the possibility or otherwise of statutes without an imperative, cp. also below, pp. 50 ff. and 103 ff.

what emerges from study and interpretation, which explains why, in historical times, the popular assemblies were largely precluded from dealing with such matters. They had to be left to the pontiffs, magistrates and senate.

The kind of question behind these rules is still extant in the Digest, for instance, where somebody asks the Republican jurist Alfenus what, if a certain legal dilemma arises, *se facere oporteret*, 'it would be proper for him to do',[1] or whether, under a certain *lex locationis*, an arrangement concerning the building of a house, *factum opus an etiam imperfectum metiri oporteret*, 'it was the correct procedure to measure the completed work only or each foot of stonework as it was erected'.[2] In neither case would the usual rendering 'to be under a duty' be adequate. The jurist is being consulted about rights as well as duties, in the second case—of the building—quite possibly by both parties together or by the judge. (To this use of *oportere* as covering rights I shall come back presently.) What is expected from him is instruction as to the course indicated by an inquiry into the law on the matter and any circumstances of legal relevance. Just so the statutes under notice satisfy a request for instruction as to the results of an inquiry into sacred wisdom.

There are preserved two senatusconsults where the senate's conclusion is expressed by means of *oportet*, and here, too, the phrase introduces a recognized standard. One dates from 159 B.C. It is the reply given the Tiburtines by some praetor in the name of the senate, to assure them that they are not deemed to have violated their covenant with Rome. It ends: 'And since you are cleared in the eyes of the senate, we believe—and it is proper for you to take the view, *vosque animum inducere oportet*— that you will also be cleared in the eyes of the Roman people'.[3] The clause deals with the problem, which seems to have worried the Tiburtines, whether a declaration of friendship by the senate is valid for the people. (It has not received sufficient attention from writers on the history of this problem.) The Tiburtines are told that 'it is proper' for them to be confident—

---

[1] D. 6. 1. 58.   [2] 19. 2. 30. 3.
[3] Bruns, 171. I am slightly modernizing the spelling.

scil. considering the constitutional practice in these matters. Constitutional practice is the authority on which, in the senate's opinion, they may rely. It is interesting that what emerges in this case from a consideration of the standard is not only a duty, but also a concession, an assurance; *animum inducere oportet* means not only 'from our practice it follows that you must take the view', but also, and even chiefly, 'from our practice it follows that you may safely take the view'. I shall soon have to say a little more about this.

The other resolution to be adduced was directed against the tribunes belonging to Caesar's party, who prevented or vetoed any motion of the senate which favoured Pompey. It was, indeed, itself vetoed so that it never became a complete senatusconsult but remained a mere *senatus auctoritas*. It declares that, in the senate's opinion, 'none of the tribunes may properly cause delay in these affairs', *neminem moram adferre oportere.*[1] The higher authority out of respect for which they should refrain from such conduct is expressly named. It is more than constitutional practice, in fact, something overruling it—namely, the welfare of the state. The resolution adds that of anyone who does cause delay 'the senate holds that he has acted against the commonwealth'. It is almost a matter of *fas* over against *ius*. The tribunes may have the latter on their side, but a proper reading of the former shows their obstruction to be wicked. One is strongly reminded of the application of *oportet* in those early statutes where it refers to the will of the gods, except that for the religious consideration of the will of the gods we have now to substitute the more political one of the *salus reipublicae*.

Here is the place to mention a third senatusconsult—*de aedificiis non diruendis*—which uses *oportet* in its motivation, or more precisely, in the motivation of its second half.[2] The first imposes a penalty on a man who, for purpose of profit, purchases a building with a view to demolishing it. The second is directed against the vendor in such a case; it begins 'And as it is equally improper—*cumque aeque non oporteret*—to lead people

[1] Bruns, 190.   [2] Bruns, 200.

astray[1] by selling'. The governing considerations to which
oporteret alludes are fully set out in the motivation of the first
half: the interest of the emperor, Claudius, in this matter, the
peaceful aspect of the country and so forth. The words quoted
refer back to this part. We ought to paraphrase: 'And as selling
is equally improper—scil. according to the principles stated
above'.

A para-legal example is the rhetorical division of argument
into *ius*, i.e. the question whether *licuerit* or *possit*, whether
defendant was in strictness empowered to act as he did, and
aequitas, i.e. the question whether *oportuerit* or *debeat*, whether,
considering the deeper requirements of justice, he should really
have acted thus.[2] Its influence may be seen in legal texts, for
instance, in the decision that, if the husband of an adulteress is
a magistrate in office, excluded from accusation, her father
'can' but 'in all fairness may not' forestall his son-in-law.[3]

It should be noted that a true insight into the setting of
oportere will lead to the clearing up of quite a few problems
besides that with which we are immediately concerned. I will
go through the most interesting.

Oportere signifies 'it is correct, proper'. Hence it may refer,
not only to what is necessary, to duties, but also to what is
permitted, to rights. I may say 'The correct thing is to wear
evening dress', i.e. it is necessary; but I may also say, 'It is
perfectly correct to wear a lounge suit', i.e. it is permitted.
This nuance has escaped the notice of legal historians; there
is no mention of it in Heumann–Seckel's dictionary.[4] It is
obviously irreconcilable with a view which assigns to *oportet*
the primary sense of 'there is a duty', *müssen*. Certainly,
Heumann–Seckel list other meanings as well, for instance, 'it
is needful', *notwendig sein*, 'it is imperative', *geboten sein* (also
'there is need to conclude', *die Notwendigkeit eines Schlusses*,
which curious rendering I shall consider presently, in discussing

---

[1] Cp. *pessimo exemplo faenerare* in the *senatusconsultum Macedonianum* (Bruns, 203) of
about the same period.   [2] Seneca, Contr. 1. 4. 6, 1. 1. 13.
[3] D. 48. 5. 16 pr.; cp. 9. 3. 5. 12. The question of interpolation need not here
be raised.
[4] *Heumanns Handlexikon*, 9th ed. by Seckel, 1907, 393 f.

fictitious actions). But as the starting-point is wrong, the essential role and possibilities of the verb are misjudged.

I have already quoted texts where a jurist is asked about *oportere* in a very general way, about the proper course both with regard to duties and rights, and also an old senatusconsult assuring the Tiburtines that it is quite proper for them, *oportet*, to regard themselves as fully cleared.

The resolution *de imperio Vespasiani* provides that 'whatever by virtue of any statute it was proper for Augustus, Tiberius or Claudius to do, all that Vespasian may be allowed to do', *quaeque ex quaque lege Augustum facere oportuit, ea Vespasiano facere liceat*.[1] The authority determining what is 'proper' is specified— the statutes from which previous emperors derived some of their powers. But it is clear that *oportuit*, 'it was proper for them under these statutes to do certain things', is almost equivalent to *licuit*, 'they were allowed to do these things'.

From the Edict, *unde legitimi* may be adduced where a deceased person's goods are promised to him *quem heredem esse oporteret*,[2] 'who would properly be heir' if there were no will. The position of an heir involves rights and liabilities, but the stress here is manifestly on the former.

Again, Ulpian decides—or, possibly, adopts Sabinus's decision—that if a party wall was defective, *utique demolire eum oportuit*, 'it was assuredly proper to pull it down'.[3] The co-owner, that is, whose building was not sufficiently supported was entitled to take steps. But he was hardly obliged to do so. The same jurist holds that if a *dos aestimata* is evicted, *maritum agere et praestare oportet*, 'the proper course for the husband is to sue the wife and, on dissolution of the marriage, to restore to her whatever he has obtained'.[4] Beseler is rash in taking exception to the text because *oportet* covers *agere*, a right, as well as *praestare*, a duty.[5]

That *oportet* far more often denotes what is necessary than what is permitted is indisputable. In the area of law and legal

---

[1] Bruns, 203.   [2] Lenel, 356.   [3] D. 39. 2. 37 pr.   [4] D. 23. 3. 16.
[5] *Zeitschrift der Savigny-Stiftung* 45, 1925, *Rom. Abt.*, 257. There are undoubtedly some interpolations.

discussion, we could not expect anything else. Interest is here normally focused on what you must do, not on what you may. Indeed, the same is true outside the law when we concern ourselves with the conduct befitting a situation.

It may also be admitted that even when *oportet* refers to rights, it does not express a complete freedom of choice. 'The proper' always retains a trace of 'the requisite'. This is obvious in the cases where a jurist is asked for advice as to the *oportere* in a problematic position, i.e. as to the entire complex of rights and duties. But it is noticeable in all other cases as well. When Ulpian says of a defective wall that 'it was proper to demolish it', though he may not think of a legal obligation, he does imply that the circumstances were such as to call for demolition. The Tiburtines are not only encouraged to feel safe; it would be wrong, offensive, if they doubted the efficacy of the senatus-consult. Even the resolution concerning Vespasian, where *oportuit* is taken up by *liceat*, contemplates official acts, which are the duty and not only the right of the Emperor. In constitutional law a legal right tends to be a moral duty—for example, the citizen's right to vote and the King's right to dissolve Parliament.

None the less, when these reservations are made, the fact remains that only by turning to the basic meaning of *oportet*, 'it is proper, correct', can we understand why it does sometimes cover what is permitted.

It is only in this way that we shall understand the full significance of *oportere* in the formula. *Oportet* means 'it is proper', scil. according to a recognized standard. When a plaintiff claims that 'it is proper for defendant to pay', *dare oportere*, or when the formula tells the judge to condemn defendant if it appears that 'it is proper for him to pay', this, originally at least, is not a vague reference to some duty. The plaintiff's assertion, which the judge is asked to investigate, means that a consideration of the law, or of legally valid transactions—say, a testament or a *sponsio*—will prove defendant under an obligation. 'It is correct for defendant to pay' means 'From a reading of the judicially relevant facts it follows that defendant must pay'.

A formula like the Publician is simply incapable of a reasonable translation unless we take *oportere*, not in the sense of
'to be under a duty', but in that of 'it is correct in view of
the legal position'. *Si quem hominem Aulus Agerius emit anno
possedisset, tum si eum hominem eius esse oporteret, condemna*:[1] this
is an order to condemn if, had the year of usucapion been
completed, 'it would be the correct decision' that the slave
was plaintiff's.

We can go further. It is this connexion of *oportere* with the
interpretation of law, this use of the term as referring to a
higher authority, an accepted standard, which must be considered the deeper cause of the fact that Republican and
classical lawyers—and the praetor himself—apply the word exclusively to civil obligations, never to praetorian or aedilician.
This is not an arbitrary convention, still less an accident. The
point is that only of a civil obligation can it be affirmed that 'it
is the proper thing' in the sense of 'found due in accordance
with established principles, in accordance with the law'. But
a praetorian or aedilician obligation cannot be inferred from
a search into the law or legally recognized transactions. It has
nothing to do with interpretation, with looking to a higher
authority. It has no basis whatever beyond its realization in
the action which the magistrate may grant.

The praetor, incidentally, even outside the province of obligations, never—with one apparent exception which I shall discuss
in a subsequent lecture[2]—uses *oportere* but as signifying what is
'correct' at civil law. This is overlooked by Lenel when he
proposes the rubric: *Quibus causis praeiudicium fieri non oportet*,
'Issues that it is not correct to prejudice by decisions on minor
points'.[3] The rubric is entirely conjectural; *ne fiat*, 'Issues that
may not be prejudiced', is far more likely. Similarly, *oportebit*
in the reconstructions of *Quod quisque iuris in alterum statuerit*, 'Any
new rule laid down by a magistrate to the detriment of a party
will be enforced against himself should that party sue him',[4]
and of *Ut in possessionem esse liceat*, 'It should be permissible to be

[1] Lenel, 171.   [2] See below, pp. 97 ff.
[3] 140.   [4] 59.

in possession in order to guard a legacy',[1] is extremely doubtful. The phrase *ex edicto oportere*, tentatively suggested by Lenel in the latter case, and with no textual support, is impossible.[2] In Bruns,[3] an edictal title is introduced which is not to be found in Lenel: *Quando cum praescriptione agere oporteat*, 'When it is proper to bring an action with a *praescriptio*'. There is no evidence whatever to confirm it, and the foregoing considerations show that it cannot have run like this.

It is true that Lenel, when coining the title *Quibus causis praeiudicium fieri non oportet*, may have thought of Cicero: *non enim oportet praeiudicium fieri*, 'for it is not proper that the major issue should be prejudiced'.[4] But this is clearly given as the argument of an advocate. There is no sign that it is a quotation from the Edict. A few lines farther on, Cicero writes that 'it is proper', *oportet*, for each party to consider how and when to bring an action—another example of non-technical use. The classical jurists also do not use, or avoid, the term with the same strictness as the praetor. It would be wrong to deny the authenticity of a remark by Ulpian such as this: *legatorum nomine satisdari oportere praetor putavit*, 'the praetor found it proper that security should be given for legacies'.[5] Let us note, however, that what moved the praetor to this opinion cannot have been any rules of the Edict—they were the result of the opinion, not its basis—but the old-established, general aims of his office. So *oportere* here does not really signify what is proper in accordance with the Edict, but rather with the praetor's duty under public law.

Our thesis enables us to draw certain conclusions as to the rise of *bonae fidei iudicia*. No doubt *oportet* in legal language at first

[1] 369. In D. 36. 4. 1. 1, *quia verum est per eum cui caveri oportebit non fieri quominus caveatur* does not necessarily reflect the wording of the edict: the comprehensive *eum cui caveri oportebit* seems to include legatee and fideicommissary, while the praetor's regulation referred only to the legatee. The sentence may not even be classical; it strikes one as superfluous.

[2] *Ex edicto oportere* occurs only in what purports to be a quotation of *Quae in fraudem creditorum facta sunt*, D. 42. 8. 10 pr. It is generally recognized that the clause containing *oportere* has been interfered with by post-classical lawyers, and Lenel (497) should not have left *oportet* standing. Similarly, no reliance is to be placed on the clause with *oportere* in *Quae fraudationis causa gesta erunt* (435 f.).

[3] 218.   [4] Inv. 2. 20. 60.   [5] D. 36. 3. 1. pr.

always meant *e lege* or *more oportet*, 'it is proper because of a statute or custom', or at least *ex testamento oportet* or the like, 'it is proper because of a will or some other recognized transaction'. As a rule *e lege* or *more* would not be expressly put: everybody knew that, in the field of law, those were the standards on which any *oportere* rested. I have, however, already cited a decree (about Vespasian) where *e lege* is added, and we shall come across many more. An instructive case is *unde legitimi*. The goods of a deceased man are here promised to him 'for whom it would be proper to be heir if there were no will', *quem heredem esse oporteret*.[1] The very rubric shows that 'it would be proper' means 'it would be proper in view of the *leges*'. Moreover, there is a passage in Cicero where the clause is applied to provincials and where, therefore, the statutes to be taken into account are specified. Epicrates received a legacy from a woman who was so near a relative 'that even had she died intestate, *Epicratem Bidinorum legibus heredem esse oporteret*, it would have been right, under the statutes of Bidis, for Epicrates to be heir'.[2]

As for *more oportere*, it occurs, for instance, in a provision concerning a husband *quem more maiorum lugeri non oportet*, 'whom it is not proper to mourn in the traditional way'.[3] No mourning rites were tolerated, for example, in the case of a traitor or enemy: 'so perish every Roman woman who mourns an enemy', said Horatius, killing his sister,[4] and the senate declared it sinful to bury or mourn the soldiers put to death because they had sacked Rhegium.[5] Remember also the law of Numa, denying the rites to a man killed by lightning. Admittedly, it is probable that, in the provision quoted, *more* primarily defines, not *oportet*, but *lugeri* (and I have translated accordingly); i.e. the meaning is not 'it is by tradition improper to mourn', but 'it is improper to perform the traditional mourning'. This does not alter the fact that what is proper, or rather improper, is

[1] Lenel, 356.
[2] Verr. 2. 2. 22. 53. In 2. 1. 45. 117, *non minus multis signis quam e lege oportet* probably also signifies 'with the full number of seals required by the statute applying to the province or the parties in question'.
[3] D. 3. 2. 11. 1.
[4] Livy 1. 26. 5.
[5] Frontinus, Strat. 4. 1. 38

here expressly connected with the province of *mos*. There are a number of texts where *e lege* occupies a position similar to that of *more* here.

Lex or *mos* was the authority to which *oportere* referred. The term comes from the domain of wise counsel, of interpretation of statutes or hallowed usage.

Evidently, when, at a later date, a person might claim that another *dare oportere ex fide bona*, the phrase *ex fide bona* was replacing *e lege* or *more* (no matter whether an implied or explicit *e lege* or *more*). The new claim meant that 'it was proper for defendant to pay—not because of a statute or custom, formerly the only basis of an obligation, but—because of good faith'. It was now admitted that *bona fides* no less than *lex* or *mos*, or a transaction recognized by them such as a will, might be the authority from which it would be possible to infer 'the proper thing to do'. In other words, *bona fides* was introduced, not as a standard with the aid of which an existing obligation could be more closely circumscribed, but as a source of duties like statute or custom. This is not to deny that the new source was from the outset such that the question whether there was an obligation overlapped with the question what exactly it entailed in a much higher degree than where statute or custom were concerned.

Whether this new basis of obligations was first developed in order to extend certain branches of the law to peregrines, not covered by *lex* or *mos*, or in order to render enforceable fresh types of transactions, not covered by these, may be left open. (Similarly, we need not inquire whether the circles urging that, in addition to an *oportere ex lege*, 'the correct thing on the ground of a statute', there was an *oportere ex bona fide*, 'the correct thing on the ground of good faith', were those that clothed their transactions with the proviso *ius civile absit et dolus malus*.) The main conclusion is supported by a further consideration. Had *bona fides* been introduced as a standard with the help of which to circumscribe an existing obligation, one would expect either *ex fide bona dare oportere* or *dare ex fide bona oportere*; for it would be solely the contents of the obligation, the *dare* or *facere*, which would depend on good faith, and vary in accordance with it, not the obligation as such. However, the earliest usage is probably *dare oportere ex fide bona*. To go by Gaius, a formula *in ius concepta* runs *quidquid dare facere oportet ex fide bona*,[1] and the *lex Rubria* proposes a formula *quidquid Q. Licinium ex ea stipulatione L. Seio dare facere oporteret ex fide bona*.[2] The words *ex bona fide*, that is, relate to *oportere*. It is the obligation as such which depends on good faith—good faith is its source. Certainly, as may be gathered from other texts, the order of words is not decisive.[3] But it does provide some slight corroboration.

Form criticism in this case confirms a result already reached by a different route. The view here taken of the original role of *bona fides* is adumbrated in a remark by Lenel;[4] and it was fully worked out by Kunkel shortly before the war.[5]

It remains to add that, if we proceed from the true meaning of *oportet*, 'it is proper in view of some higher authority', 'it emerges as correct from an inquiry into the statutes and so on', all the well-known difficulties of translation and alleged discrepancies between various uses vanish. I have already pointed out that, on this basis, the Publician formula allows of a smooth rendering: 'Condemn if, had the year been completed, it would be proper for the slave to be plaintiff's', *si eum hominem eius esse oporteret*. The same is true of the formula by which a *bonorum possessor* claims property: *Si Aulus Agerius heres esset, tum si eum fundum eius esse oporteret, condemna*,[6] 'Condemn if, were plaintiff heir, it would be proper for the land to be his'. It is not accidental that *oportere* occurs only in such actions *in rem* as contain a fiction. Something stronger than *parere*, 'to appear', is here wanted to emphasize that, if only the fiction is granted, the conclusion put will indeed follow from statute or custom: not just 'if, supposing a certain element were present, it would

---

[1] 4. 47. Buckland, *Manual of Roman Private Law*, 2nd ed., 1939, 421 f., in the formulas of *actio venditi* and *actio negotiorum gestorum*, makes *ex fide bona* precede *dare facere*. (He also puts *quidquid paret oportere* instead of *quidquid oportet*.) Lenel, 299, 105, seems preferable.   [2] Bruns, 98.

[3] E.g. D. 44. 7. 5 pr., G. 3. 137, 4. 61, D. 44. 7. 2. 3, G. 2. 213, 4. 55, D. 30. 82. 1.   [4] 4, n. 1.   [5] *Festschrift Koschaker*, 1939, vol. ii, 1 ff.

[6] Lenel, 183.

appear', but 'if, supposing the element were present, it would be the correct thing on the ground of *lex* or *mos*'.

What aberrations may be produced by losing sight of the basic sense of *oportere* may be gathered from the discussion of fictitious actions *in personam* in Heumann–Seckel's dictionary.[1] To take *actio furti* as example, the ordinary action directs the judge to condemn 'if it appears that defendant has committed the theft for which defendant *damnum decidere oportet*';[2] a fictitious action—against a peregrine—orders condemnation 'if it appears that defendant has committed the theft for which defendant, were he a citizen, *damnum decidere oporteret*'.[3] The dictionary maintains that, in analogy to fictitious actions *in rem*, strictly, a fictitious *actio furti* should read: 'for which defendant *damnum decidere oportere oporteret*'. The shorter 'for which *damnum decidere oporteret*', we are told, is only a contraction, though a natural one.

Needless to say, there is no trace of *oportere oporteret* in any text, legal or lay. This eccentric combination[4] could be proposed only so long as, fundamentally, *oportere* was equated with 'to be under a duty', no attention being paid to its essential setting in life. Then it proved impossible to reconcile the Publician formula with the general meaning of the term; a secondary one was invented, 'there is need to conclude'; and the Publician was translated by 'if, had the year elapsed, there would be need to conclude that the slave was plaintiff's'. In analogy, a fictitious action *in personam* was thought of as dealing with a theft 'for which, were he a citizen, there would be need to conclude (*oporteret*) that defendant was under a duty (*oportere*) to pay a penalty'.

But all this is wrong. How should *oportet*—*oportet* alone, not *oportet concludere*—come to signify 'there is need to conclude'? (Which, be it noted, is very different from 'it is proper', even though what is proper can be established only by reasoning from a standard.) Why should this strange sense appear exclusively in fictitious actions and nowhere else in Latin literature? If this strange sense were intended, would it be so natural

---

[1] Loc. cit. (s.v. *oportere*).   [2] Lenel, 328.   [3] Lenel, 324.
[4] One is reminded of the ἀδολεσχεῖν of De Sophisticis Elenchis.

to obscure it in actions *in personam* by putting *oporteret* instead of *oportere oporteret*? Clearly, the Publician formula must be rendered 'if, had the year elapsed, it would be proper for the slave to be plaintiff's'; and the fictitious action *in personam* 'if it appears that defendant has committed a theft for which, were he a citizen, it would be proper for him—scil. under the XII Tables —to pay a penalty'. The ordinary action *in personam* asserts that 'it is proper for him', the fictitious that, if a certain element were present, 'it would be proper'. There is nothing to suggest a contraction from *oportere oporteret*. In fact, the interpretation 'there would be need to conclude that he is under a duty' runs counter both to the evidence and to philological principles, while the phrase 'it would be proper for it to be proper for him' would be senseless.

It is not easy for the current doctrine to explain the relation between the use of *oportere* as referring to a private law duty and its use as referring to a public law duty; and some passages where these uses are mixed up prove rather troublesome. No discrepancy remains once it is realized that *oportere* primarily denotes, not 'a duty', but 'the correct thing in view of statutes and custom'. It may be statutes and custom dealing with private law, or statutes and custom dealing with public law, or some of the former kind and some of the latter at the same time. A person's claim that another *dare oportere*, that 'it is proper for defendant to pay', would normally rest on a statute concerning private law. The *lex Papiria de sacramentis*, according to which the *tresviri capitales* are to exact *sacramenta* and give judgment 'as it is proper for them to do by virtue of statutes and plebiscites', *uti ex legibus plebeique scitis exigere iudicareque oportet*,[1] no doubt means both statutes concerning private law and statutes concerning public law; and so does, for instance, the senatusconsult permitting Vespasian to do 'whatever under any statute it was proper, *oportuit*, for previous emperors to do'.

An important point to notice is that, in some respects, the distinction between private and public law is artificial. Above all, any legislation concerning the former automatically

[1] Bruns, 47.

produces duties in the field of the latter, in that it imposes the task of giving it effect on whoever is entrusted with jurisdiction. That is to say, if it is 'proper' for a citizen to pay a debt—a duty at private law—or acquire an inheritance—a right at private law—it is also 'proper' for the magistrate or judge to see that he pays or acquires—a duty at public law. Accordingly, we find the praetor promising: *Uti me quaque lege senatusconsulto bonorum possessionem dare oportebit, ita dabo,*[1] 'As it will be correct for me, in pursuance of any statute or senatusconsult, to grant possession of an estate, so I shall grant it'. He has in mind laws creating private law rights, yet he speaks of 'the proper course for him', a public law duty. (Maybe the particular laws in question were more immediately addressed to him than others; not 'this or that person is to obtain the goods', but 'the praetor is to give them to this or that person'.) In *unde legitimi*, the emphasis remains on the other side. The estate is promised to him *quem heredem esse oporteret*, 'for whom it would be proper to be heir' in the absence of a will. In a divisory action, the judge must allot to each party *quantum adiudicari oportet*,[2] 'as much as it is proper to allot'. Here *oportet* plainly signifies both what is 'proper' for each party, as a private law right, and what is 'proper' for the judge, as a public law duty.

None of these cases creates the slightest difficulty provided we start, not from 'to be under a duty', but from 'to be the correct thing'. There are many instances of a law referring to 'the correct thing by virtue of statutes etc.', *oportere e legibus, plebiscitis, senatusconsultis,*[3] all easily understandable on this basis. A *lex agraria* of 111 B.C. considers him *cuius eum agrum ex lege plebeive scito esse oportet oportebitve,*[4] 'to whom it is, or will be, the correct thing, on the ground of a statute, for that land to belong', or *quem in viasieis ex senatusconsulto esse oportet oportebitve,*[5] 'for whom it is or will be proper, on the ground of a senatusconsult, to

---

[1] Lenel, 360.   [2] Lenel, 208, 211.

[3] E.g. *lex Papiria de sacramentis* (Bruns, 47), *lex Cornelia de XX quaestoribus* (89 ff.), *lex Antonia de Termessibus* (92 ff.), *lex Rubria* (97 ff.), *fragmentum Atestinum* (101 f.), *tabula Heracleensis* (102 ff.), *lex Ursonensis* (122 ff.), *lex Malacitana* (147 ff.), *senatus-consultum de imperio Vespasiani* (202 f.), *edictum Augusti de aquaeductu Venafrano* (249 ff.)

[4] Bruns, 75, section 9.   [5] Bruns, 75, section 12.

live near a highway'. There is no inconsistency between the two passages, though there would be a formidable one if we rendered *oportere* as 'to be under a duty'; the former clause would actually become untranslatable. Again, it is very usual for a statute, when coming back in a later chapter to an institution set up by an earlier, to describe it as an institution which *hac lege*—or *ex hac lege*—*oportebit*, which 'will be the correct thing under this statute'. In what is left of the *lex agraria* just mentioned alone, there are nearly twenty such passages,[1] where, clearly, the orthodox interpretation of *oportere* will not do.

Its inadequacy comes out in a typical way in the prevalent treatment of the familiar maxim, which Gaius ascribes to the early jurists, that *ante litem contestatam dare debitorem oportere, post litem contestatam condemnari oportere, post condemnationem iudicatum facere oportere.*[2] Modern authorities constantly try to get something of the meaning 'to be under a duty' into *condemnari oportere*. Wenger proposes *der Beklagte muss jetzt den Prozess über sich ergehen lassen*,[3] Buckland 'the defendant is now bound to submit to judgment'.[4] But this is obviously forced, and it puts us on the wrong track. The true sense is: 'Before *litiscontestatio* it is the proper thing—scil. in view of statutes and custom—for defendant to pay, afterwards it is the proper thing for him to be condemned, and after condemnation it is the proper thing for him to satisfy the judgment.' As for duties, the main duty implied in *debitorem condemnari oportere* is definitely the judge's, not the debtor's. Of course, the latter is 'held fast'—*tenetur* in Gaius's language—throughout the three stages.

C. Separation and Combination of Rule and Sanction

To go on to my third question. When does a lawgiver separate command or prohibition and sanction—'This or that

---

[1] See also, e.g., *lex Latina tabulae Bantinae* (Bruns, 53 ff.), *lex Acilia repetundarum* (55 ff.), *tabula Heracleensis* (102 ff.), *lex Quinctia de aquaeductibus* (113 ff.), *fragmentum Florentinum* (117 f.), *lex Ursonensis* (122 ff.), *lex Salpensana* (142 ff.), *lex Malacitana* (147 ff.), *fragmentum Tudertinum* (157 f.).   [2] G. 3. 180.

[3] *Institutionen des römischen Zivilprozessrechts*, 1925, 169. In English, 'the defendant must now put up with the suit': *Institutes of the Roman Law of Civil Procedure*, transl. by Fisk, 1940, pp. 180 f.

[4] *Main Institutions*, 1931, 366.

shall, or shall not, be done; whoever disobeys will suffer for it'—
and when does he combine them—'Whoever acts, or does not
act, in this or that way will suffer for it'? Once again it is
not blind chance that determines the election. For surely, if it
is absolutely clear, even before the lawgiver speaks, where
your duty lies, it would be absurd to issue a solemn order and
then only add the penalty in the event of transgression; and if
what he requires of you, though not quite so self-evident, yet contains nothing surprising or intricate, to have a special command
or prohibition precede the sanction is at least unnecessary.
Remember that I am dealing with early, unsophisticated legislation. There came a period in Talmudic law when it was assumed
that the Bible had two separate statutes for each crime, one to
prohibit it and one to lay down the penalty.

It would, then, be absurd for a lawgiver to say: 'Murder is
forbidden: if anyone violates this decree, he shall be put to
death.' The sensible form in this case is the other, which, so
to speak, takes the prohibition of murder for granted and concentrates on making clear what will happen if you disregard it:
'If a man murders another man, he shall be put to death.' Or
take a notice directed against bathing in a lake. This is capable
of either formulation. It may be treated as a novel thing and be
framed very precisely: 'Bathing prohibited. Anyone disregard-
ing this notice will be fined £10.' But a prohibition of this kind
is so little surprising and complicated that the combined form
also suffices: 'Anyone bathing in this lake will be fined £10.'
As you know, both types of notices are frequent—too frequent
for our liking.

On the other hand, where a duty to be imposed is new, un-
expected or complicated, the natural course a lawgiver will
adopt is first to explain what he wants and to proclaim the
sanction by way of an appendix. Mr. Strachey was wise in not
rushing upon us with 'If a baker sells, or a customer buys, more
than a small loaf for 2 BUs, or more than a large loaf for 4, or
more than ½lb. of buns for 1, and so on, he shall be liable to
this or that penalty.' His was not a simple, obvious demand. So
he started by putting his exact wishes, and then, in a final

paragraph, supported them by the usual threats. Similarly, when two states conclude a detailed treaty, we shall expect them first to set down the various rights and duties of each and then to attach a sanction; it would not do to say 'If this state does not do so and so, and the other does not do so and so, and again if the former does so and so and the latter so and so—then the party concerned is to incur punishment.' In Ivanhoe, the Grand Master declares:[1] 'Rebecca, in those lists shalt thou produce thy champion; and if thou failest to do so, thou shalt die the death of a sorceress.' A contraction of the two distinct provisions into one, 'Rebecca, if thou failest to produce thy champion in those lists, thou shalt die', would rob the former of much of its weight as a novel, exceptional and final decision.

If this is correct, if the two forms reflect different settings in life, then, by paying attention to them, we may learn more about the evolution of some laws than would emerge from a mere consideration of their matter. Let us return to the examples from the Edict I mentioned. 'Whoever publicly rails at a man in an objectionable manner,' says the praetor, 'against him I shall give an action.' It would have been superfluous to issue a separate injunction, 'Public insults in an objectionable manner are not permitted.' For one thing, the offence had been punishable ever since the XII Tables.[2] For another, who had the slightest doubt, quite apart from any legal precepts, that this was a wrong thing to do? Again, there is an edict, 'If anyone accosts a matron in an objectionable manner, I shall take steps.' Here also no special decree was needed saying 'Nobody may behave improperly to a matron.' Everybody knew that such conduct was reprehensible, and in any case, it was easy to infer that much from the praetor's warning, 'If anyone misbehaves in this indecent way, I shall take steps.'

When we come to the next rule, however, the position is different. 'Nothing may be done on purpose to bring infamy on a man.' This time we find an express prohibition, and after it

---

[1] 2. 15.   [2] VIII 1. See Daube, *Cambridge Law Journal* 7, 1939, 46.

only the praetor goes on: 'If anyone acts contrary to this, I shall inquire into the case.' The form suggests, what in this instance we are able to check with the help of external evidence, that the provision constituted a fresh departure.[1] It was, indeed, a bold step on the praetor's part when he announced that acts, otherwise perfectly in order, would be deemed unlawful if done with a view to making a man infamous. And that is what he meant. It was, for example, perfectly in order for you to walk next to me in the street in mourning and unshaven. But from now, you might not do it if you intended thereby to indicate that I had treated you in a dastardly fashion. There had been nothing remotely approaching this regulation in the older law. Nor was the praetor unaware of the danger of abuse. That is why he promised, not an immediate action as for instance in the case of railing at a man, but only an inquiry; i.e. actions would be granted sparingly, on very careful examination. Later on, when the scope of the edict was sufficiently fixed through continuous application, and abuse appeared less likely, a person whom another had tried to render infamous could at once ask for an action on the ground of outrage, an *actio iniuriarum*. But from one of Seneca's Controversiae[2] we may see that even then the more conservative minds opposed the relaxation. It was, then, in promulgating that revolutionary ordinance that the praetor placed in front an express prohibition, 'Nothing may be done on purpose to bring infamy on a man', attaching the sanction in an additional clause, 'If anyone acts contrary to this, I shall inquire into the matter.'

Just so, if we compare *De his qui deiecerint* and *Ne quis in suggrunda*,[3] we notice that the two pronouncements start from different presuppositions. The former simply promises an action against the occupier of a dwelling from which things are thrown to the damage of a passer. It does not say that things must not be thrown—it is so obvious. The latter, on the other hand, opens by forbidding the keeping of things on one's roof to the

---

[1] See Daube, *Essays Presented to J. H. Hertz*, 1942, 111 ff., and *Atti del Congresso Internazionale di Diritto Romano, Verona 1948*, vol. iii, 1951, 413 ff.   [2] 5. 30.
[3] Lenel, 173 f. The two formed a single edict; see 174, n. 3.

danger of passers; and only then does it promise an action against him who violates the decree. Clearly, at the time, it was far from obvious that you could not store things in whatever manner you liked. *De feris*, the edict of the aediles against keeping wild beasts by the wayside to the danger of the public,[1] shows the structure of *Ne quis in suggrunda*: first the prohibition, then, separately, the sanction in case any harm is done. Nowadays the other structure would be more appropriate. Its form indicates that when the edict was first published, it imposed a quite new restriction.

The *lex Quinctia de aquaeductibus*[2] uses both forms. It lays down, first, that 'whoever damages an aqueduct shall pay so and so much and repair it'; secondly, that 'if an enclosure around an aqueduct is marked off, no one shall build or plant within it; whoever does, to him the same rules shall apply as to one who causes damage'. That you may not damage an aqueduct is taken for granted; that you may not build or plant within the enclosure needs to be specially stated.

Livy's account of the *leges Valeriae Horatiae* of 449 B.C. is significant—no matter whether or not we regard it as historically trustworthy.[3] Of one statute he assumes that it was new when enacted, and this puts first a prohibition and then the sanction: 'No one may create a magistrate against whose sentence there is no appeal even if it is capital; he who does so may be killed without offence to the law.' Another statute (as he sees it) merely underlined the sacrosanctity of the tribunes which had long been recognized. Here we find only a sanction, the prohibition being taken for granted: 'He who hurts the tribunes, his head shall be forfeited to Jupiter.'

Two paragraphs from Cato may also be adduced.[4] He draws up a model contract between the owner of an olive grove and a person undertaking to gather the olives for him. The following terms occur: 'Ladders are to be returned in the same condition as they were given; if they are not so returned, a deduction will be made. If any damage is done to the owner through the contractor's fault, a deduction will be made.' In the second

---

[1] Lenel, 566.   [2] Bruns, 113.   [3] 3. 55. 5, 7.   [4] R.R. 144. 3.

provision, the sanction alone is stated. There is no need for an express clause: 'The contractor shall do the owner no damage.'

The thesis I am advancing has a bearing on the very opening of the XII Tables. I have pointed out that if it is quite clear where your duty lies, an ancient lawgiver will not expressly repeat it and then attach a separate sanction, but will take it for granted and state the sanction only. He will not say 'Do this—if you do not, the consequences will be such and such', but simply 'If you do not do this, the consequences will be such and such.' The very beginning of the XII Tables, however, seems to contradict this proposition: *Si in ius vocat ito; ni it antestamino*,[1] 'If there is a summons to appear before the court, the person summoned shall go; if he does not go, the summoner shall call witnesses.' Surely, that you ought to comply with a summons to court was not in doubt. The XII Tables, with their particularly terse style, would not have troubled about an established rule like this. Their aim in this section was to define and limit the rights of the summoner if his request was disregarded.

Now the fragment is preserved in Porphyrio, but in a corrupt state, as follows: *Si in ius vocat ionitantestamin*. When we count the letters in *ionitantestamin*, we find that there are fifteen, whereas the current restoration *ito ni it antestamino* contains eighteen. Moreover, it is precisely the letters *i*, *o*, and *t*, making *ito*, which are arbitrarily added. The conclusion is obvious. The XII Tables opened: *Si in ius vocat, ni it, antestamino*. The duty to follow the summons was implied, order and sanction in the event of disobedience were given in one. The structure of this law was exactly parallel to the well-known *Si intestato moritur, cui suus heres nec escit, adgnatus proximus familiam habeto*,[2] 'If a man dies intestate, and he has no child to be his heir, the nearest agnate shall have the estate.' Both provisions begin by putting the general situation, a summons before the court or the death of a person who has made no will; both take the normal legal consequence for granted, that the person summoned should

---

[1] Bruns, 17.   [2] Bruns, 23.

obey or that the deceased should be succeeded by a child;
and both, therefore, before stating their regulation, insert a
negative condition, namely, that the normal consequence does
not follow, that the person summoned does not obey or that
there is no child to succeed. It is only for this problematic
case that the lawgiver deems it necessary to legislate. It is
noteworthy that Mommsen declared 'mihi *ito* videtur rectius
abesse'.[1]

It may be well to add a warning. In judging whether a given
senatusconsult employs one form or the other, it is important
to remember that, as senatusconsults are addressed, not to the
people at large, but to magistrates, their language and arrangement are very free in comparison with statutes and edicts. One
consequence is that, even if the main operative part introduced
by *placere* consists in a sanction only, it does not always follow
that there is no express command or prohibition: this may be
contained in the motivation introduced by *cum*.

For example, a senatusconsult *de aedificiis non diruendis*[2] in the
main part enjoins that 'if anyone for purpose of profit buys a
building with a view to pulling it down, he should pay a fine
of double the price'. At first sight, we seem to have before us
prohibition and sanction in one. But the motivation preceding
the main part gives what amounts to an explicit, separate
prohibition of such purchases: 'Since all ought to abstain from
this monstrous way of making profits.' That we must treat the
motivation and the principal rule as being on the same level,
the former putting the prohibition and the latter the sanction,
is confirmed by a further senatusconsult on the matter, passed
some ten years later.[3] It makes reference to the earlier decree
and says that, by the earlier one, 'it was provided that no one
might buy a building to be pulled down for purpose of profit,
and a penalty was imposed on a purchaser acting contrary to
the senatusconsult'. Clearly, for the author of this second

[1] Bruns, 18 note on I 1. Incidentally, though it is certain that the XII Tables
had the old imperative *antestamino*, not the plural *antestamini* which would not fit
at all, Porphyrio or his source did write *antestamini*, more familiar by then. What is
extant is *antestaminigitur*, plainly a case of haplography, one *i* instead of two.

[2] Bruns, 200.   [3] Bruns, 201.

senatusconsult, the first showed the form separating prohibition
and sanction. The point made in the motivation—'since all
ought to abstain'—counts as a full prohibition.

This being so, the question is justified whether, say, in the
case of the *senatusconsultum Macedonianum*,[1] we should not also
construe the motivation as containing a prohibition: 'Since he
who lends money (scil. to a *filiusfamilias*) under no specific
business headings often causes immoral characters to offend.'
Maybe in the eyes of a Roman lawyer this constituted a prohibition of such loans, and the main part of the senatusconsult,
declaring that they should not be actionable, laid down the
penalty in the event of transgression. On this assumption, the
senatusconsultum Macedonianum states prohibition and sanction
separately—an indication that the prohibition was a novel
thing at that time. In other words, the form, on this assumption,
provides some support for the view—for which there is much to
be said on other grounds—that this decree was not, as is widely
believed, preceded by very similar legislation a few years before,
but that it was the first to deal with those loans.[2]

Of course, the two forms in question—command followed
by sanction, and sanction implying the command—are only
one of many illustrations of the wider phenomenon that ancient
lawgivers do not usually state that which goes without saying.
It is well known that the praetor never promises an *actio in ius
concepta*. It would be quite unnecessary—and indeed misleading—to do so. It is enough to announce the formulas for use in
these cases.

D. *Facts Alleged and Facts Established*

We now come to the difference between 'if so and so has
occurred' and 'if so and so is alleged to have occurred'. The
latter form clearly emphasizes the doubtful quality of a matter
when it is first raised by one side. It reflects a concern with
tactics, with ways and means, with the problem whether and by
what steps the matter should be advanced or put aside. Few
statutes and senatusconsults deal with this problem. Most of

[1] Bruns, 203.
[2] See Daube, *Savigny-Stiftung* 65, 1947, *Rom. Abt.*, 308 ff. Cp. below, pp. 79, 85.

them attach consequences to facts assumed to be established:
'If a man has broken another's bone, he shall pay 300 pieces.'[1]
Similarly, the jurists try to find out, from statutes, senatusconsults and edicts, exactly what facts—established facts—should
lead to exactly what consequences. It is not, therefore, surprising
that 'if so and so is alleged' should play little part in these
branches of legal literature.

The position of praetor and aediles is radically different. In
their most creative period, it was precisely by announcing
whether and by what steps they would advance some matters
and squash others that they exercised their influence. They
did not directly legislate, attaching consequences to facts assumed
to be established; but they had power to declare which matters
might be usefully raised before them and which might not.
They were indeed concerned with tactics. Here was room,
then, for the growing up of the form: 'if so and so is alleged
to have occurred—Whatever anyone is alleged to have lent—
I shall give an action.' It is interesting that, before this form became stereotyped, a praetor might say 'if a person is brought
before me, *ad me eductus fuerit*, who is alleged to have done so and
so': 'Whoever take public contracts for clearing rivers, if any of
them is brought before me who is alleged to have contravened
the terms.'[2] The edict concentrates on the actual situation in
court when the charge is preferred.

The form is related to others reflecting the magistrate's
interest in the matter when first coming up: *si petatur*, 'if an
object is claimed', *si agatur*, 'if an action is brought'. It is in
fact more logical than the simple 'if so and so has occurred,
I shall give an action'. The latter, taken at its face value, makes
the establishment of the principal facts into a prerequisite for
an action. In strictness, the promise of an action 'if expense has
been incurred' would mean that expense must be established
beforehand and that, once an action is granted, it can no longer
be called in question. We know that such is not the meaning of

[1] Bruns, 29.
[2] Gellius 11. 17. 2. See Erman, *Savigny-Stiftung* 11, 1890, *Rom. Abt.*, 244; also
below, pp. 101 ff.

the announcement. How, then, are we to account for the
illogicality? Why does the magistrate use 'if so and so has
occurred' as well as 'if so and so is alleged'?

'If so and so has occurred' is perfectly appropriate to statutes
and senatusconsults attaching consequences to facts assumed to
be established: 'If a man has broken another's bone, he shall
be fined.' Occasionally the magistrate also, instead of or prior
to announcing the remedy he will grant, announces his ultimate
aim: 'Whatever has been done under duress I shall not uphold.'[1]
In these cases a reference to allegation, 'Whatever is alleged
to have been done under duress', would be out of place. The
point is that when a magistrate omits this reference though
logic would require it, he is glancing at the consequences to
come about should the facts alleged prove true. As he deals with
the remedy, he ought logically to say: 'If expense is alleged to
have occurred, I shall give an action.' But as he thinks of the
main purpose of his remedy, namely, condemnation of defendant and recovery by plaintiff should expense have been incurred, he puts it illogically: 'If expense has been incurred,
I shall give an action.' The illogicality betrays the presence,
behind the procedural façade, of a legislative attitude: 'If
expense has been incurred, defendant should reimburse plaintiff.'

This analysis is confirmed by the preference the magistrate
shows for one form or the other in certain cases. I have already
mentioned that where he announces his ultimate aim, thus
openly approaching the position of a lawgiver—'Whatever has
been done under duress I shall not uphold'—the reference to
allegation is never to be found. Incidentally, even the promise
of the *actio in quadruplum* in the event of duress no doubt ran:
'Whatever has been done under duress, I shall give an action.'
Lenel gives the choice between this and 'Whatever is alleged to
have been done.'[2] But the texts, among them Cicero, speak
strongly against the latter alternative, and the analogy of the
actio doli which Lenel probably has in mind—'Whatever is
alleged to have been done by fraud'—is inconclusive: there is no
near-legislative 'I shall not uphold' to open the chapter on *dolus*.

[1] Lenel, 110.   [2] 111.

Another case where, significantly, we never meet with the reference to allegation is the promise of a remedy following directly upon a command. 'Whoever sell slaves should inform the buyers of defects' is followed by 'If a slave has been sold in contravention of this, we shall give an action.'[1] Or to take a prohibition: 'No one may keep an object over a road to the danger of passers' is followed by 'Whoever has acted in contravention of this, I shall give an action against him.'[2] The legislative impulse is carried over from the command to the promise of an action. The idea of suppressing transgressions—transgressions assumed to be established—is too strong to allow of the logically correct 'Whoever is alleged to have acted in contravention.'

Conversely, the reference to allegation is particularly common in subsections. The praetor starts by saying,[3] 'From whatever house anything has been thrown down, I shall give an action against its occupant for damages': no reference to allegation, the praetor's final object—condemnation on proof of the offence—is in the foreground. Then comes a clause: 'If a free man is alleged to have perished, I shall give an action for a fine.' Here, where a complication is considered, the calmer, more logical wording is chosen. The praetor here is more conscious of the possibility of argument and counter-argument, of the litigious nature of any submission by one party. Even where a command forms the beginning and where, as we saw, the promise of a remedy immediately following it never contains the reference to allegation, any further promise for a special contingency usually does contain it. 'Whoever sell slaves should inform buyers of defects' is followed by 'If a slave has been sold in contravention of this, we shall give an action.' But in their last provision, directed against a sale which, while superficially in order, violates the spirit of their edict, the aediles say: 'All the more, if anyone is alleged to have sold in fraudulent contravention of this, we shall give an action.' Similarly, we find 'No one may keep an object to the danger of passers', followed by 'Whoever has acted in contra-

---

[1] Lenel, 555.   [2] Lenel, 174.   [3] Lenel, 173.

vention of this, I shall give an action against him.' But to this a subordinate case is added: 'If a slave is alleged to have done it.'

This is not to maintain that the opposite never happens, though I can recall only one instance: 'Through whose-ever *dolus* a sepulchre is alleged to have been violated, I shall give an action against him for damages. If anyone has made his habitation in a sepulchre, I shall give an action for a fine.'[1] There may be an explanation of the unusual diction. The main case, violation of a grave, occurs in many inscriptions, a penalty being imposed by the founder. The special case, of a grave being turned into a residence, does not seem to be represented in inscriptions at all. That is to say, in granting an action in the main case, the praetor merely sanctioned an existing usage; it was in the rarer, subordinate case that he innovated—hence the legislative nuance.

What is the relation in time between 'if so and so has occurred, I shall give an action' and 'if so and so is alleged'? Maybe the two are equally old. If not, the former, less accurate wording is probably the older.[2] Had there been a time when the magistrate used only 'if so and so is alleged to have occurred', the less accurate wording would hardly have come up. But it is easy to see how, as the magistrate became more and more aware of the precise nature of his task and the means at his disposal, the characteristic 'if so and so is alleged' developed in addition to 'if so and so has occurred'. True, it is arguable that the logical form came first and the less logical is a relaxation, or even an expression of an increase in the powers of the magistrate. But it does not seem likely.

At any rate, the question has little bearing on the dating of individual edicts. For, whatever the relative age of the forms as such, once they were both in existence, either might be employed in a fresh case. The latest edict, therefore, might yet show the earlier form; the earliest extant might show the later. All we can do is to see how far the way the magistrate chooses

---

[1] Lenel, 228.
[2] Cp. Dernburg, quoted by Karlowa, *Römische Rechtsgeschichte*, vol. i, 1885, 467, n. 1.

between the two forms sheds light on their original settings—
the one, 'if so and so is alleged', typically tactical, concerned
with the encouragement of this request and the discourage-
ment of that, the other, 'if so and so has occurred', closer to
legislation proper, glancing at the ultimate object pursued.
Even in this modest undertaking we must exercise care. One
magistrate may be less sensitive to form than another. Or
special considerations may come in: *Si mensor falsum modum
dixerit*[1] sounds better than *dixisse dicetur*.

If a digression be permissible—a *demonstratio* runs: *Quod
vendidit*, 'Whereas plaintiff has sold.' It looks like a recital of
admitted facts, but it is not; defendant is free to deny the
contract. Most modern writers adhere to one of two views. (1)
At first *demonstratio* served to submit to arbitration a mere
question of valuation; it became illogical only when a *condemnatio* was added. (2) *Quod* should here be translated by 'in
so far as', 'if'.[2] Either doctrine is tenable. I incline, however,
to put up with the illogicality as original. The *demonstratio*, as
far as form is concerned, accepts plaintiff's statement. This is
natural: it is he who will take the initiative in setting out the
principal facts and, for him, they are indeed facts, not mere
assertions. Their controversial character is brought out, as
regards form, by way of an afterthought, reflecting defendant's
objections: by *si non paret absolve*, 'if it does not so appear,
absolve', and also perhaps a little before, by *qua de re agitur*, 'about
which matter an action is brought'. In other words, contrary
to (1), *demonstratio* always figured in formulas with *condemnatio*,
and the facts in it could always be disproved; as far as its
effect is concerned, it always contained a condition. But,
contrary to (2), *quod* is put not because it means 'in so far as'
or 'if', but because the *demonstratio*, illogically, looks at the
affair through the eyes of plaintiff—or at least looked at it
through his eyes when first introduced.

So far we have proceeded from the assumption that 'if so and
so is alleged to have occurred' is alien to the style of statutes,
senatusconsults and jurists. As remarked above, there are

---

[1] Lenel, 219.   [2] Arango-Ruiz is the protagonist of (1), Koschaker of (2).

apparent exceptions. As for the jurists, it is generally recognized that this phrasing is evidence of quotation. When Ulpian says, 'If religious ground is alleged to have been sold as secular, the praetor gives an action', he must be following the Edict.[1] We may, therefore, confine ourselves to statutes and senatusconsults.

Three passages of the *lex Acilia* are credited with this form, but they are all due to conjecture.[2] The *fragmentum Atestinum* contains it in an enumeration of actions which need not go to Rome.[3] For one thing, however, their descriptions are modelled on, if not simply taken over from, the Edict. For another, the fragment comes from a *lex data*: it is itself semi-edictal. There remain two cases with the active 'if a man alleges so and so', instead of 'if so and so is alleged'. It may well be yet another more vivid precursor of the sedate, stereotyped form. (We have already mentioned 'if a man is brought before me who is alleged to have done so and so'.) It is worth noting that even the praetor, in speaking of a controversial allegation made outside his court, uses the active: 'If a widow alleges that she is with child, she should inform those whom the matter affects.'[4] The two cases are the senatusconsult *de Bacchanalibus* and the *lex Ursonensis*. The senatusconsult demands that 'if there are any who allege that they need a Bacchanal, they should approach the praetor.'[5] The provision is concerned with tactics: it states the course to be taken by private persons whose allegation has not yet even reached the authorities. Moreover, their proper course consists in approaching the praetor—there is an implied assurance that their petition will receive attention. What is most significant, however, it that the passage occurs in a part of the senatusconsult intended to be published as an edict. The case is in perfect harmony with our results. So is the *lex Ursonensis*. It includes a regulation 'if someone alleges a decurion to be unfit'.[6] This, too, is about procedure: the *duumvir iure dicundo* is enjoined to grant an action. And, as in the case of the *fragmentum Atestinum*, we have to do with a *lex data*, which is semi-edictal.

---

[1] Lenel, 227.   [2] Bruns, 59, l. 5, 71, ll. 74, 81.   [3] Bruns, 109, ll. 2 f.
[4] Lenel, 312.   [5] Bruns, 165, l. 4.   [6] Bruns, 134, ll. 20 f.

3. 'No one should wish to have offended'

By now, I like to think, you will admit that the form critical method may be of some value for elucidating the development of Roman legislation. So next, I propose to analyse a more difficult case: *Ne quis fecisse velit*, 'No one should wish to have done so and so.' It may be found, for example, in the edict recommended by the senate after the exposure of the Bacchanal societies: *Sacra in occulto ne quisquam fecisse vellet*, 'No one should wish to have performed secret rites.'[1]

No doubt philologists are right in explaining the perfect infinitive here as coming down from an infinitive with aoristic force.[2] *Nolito edepol devellisse* in Plautus[3] means 'begad, just deign not to pluck them', *devellisse* being equivalent to *devellere*. What is far from clear, however, is whether in the legal prohibitions with which we are concerned the aoristic sense is still prevalent.

Suppose it were, we must translate 'No one should wish to do so and so', as if we had before us the more familiar *ne quis facere velit*, with the action to be prohibited expressed by means of the present infinitive; and we should be approaching *noli facere*, 'Do not wish to do so and so.' But these modes of prohibition, which are particularly urbane, are not reconcilable with the spirit of legislation. *Noli, obsecro, istum disturbare*, 'Do not wish, pray, to disarrange that circle', is said by Archimedes, the civilized scholar, to his barbarian murderer;[4] and *Noli me tangere*, 'Do not wish to touch me', by the risen Jesus to Mary

---

[1] Bruns, 165; *vellet* in the imperfect because the provisions are governed by *edicendum esse censuere*. Ihering (*Geist des römischen Rechts*, 6th and 7th ed., 1923, vol. ii, pt. 2, 608, n. 828) took *nequis adiese velet* in l. 7 of the senatusconsult as standing for *nequis adesse vellet*, instead of *nequis adiisse vellet* (given by Bruns, 165, n. 9). Apart from the fact that the latter is confirmed by *nisei pr. urbanum adiesent* in l. 8, it alone is consistent with the remaining provisions. But Ihering, like the modern editors who have the correct verb and tense, attached no significance to the difference between *ne quis fecisse velit* and *ne quis facere velit*.

[2] C. E. Bennett, *Syntax of Early Latin*, vol. i, 1910, 427 f.

[3] Poen. 872.   [4] Valerius Maximus 8. 7, ext. 7.

Magdalene[1]—it is also the humble request of a lamp placed in
a grave in the Esquiline necropolis.[2] The nearest English prohibition is 'Would people—or: Would you—please not do so
and so'.

It is, indeed, conceivable that *ne quis facere velit* or *fecisse velit*,
or *noli facere* or *fecisse*, was occasionally used to refer to attempt,
or to stress the presumptuous character of the deed in question.
Velle can signify something like 'to try' or 'to dare'. There are
inscriptions of the type: 'If any try—or, dare—to sell this
monument, *si qui vendere volent*,[3] it shall belong to the munici-
pality', or 'Whoever may have tried—or, dared—to give it
away, *quisquis tradidisse voluerit*,[4] shall pay a fine.' Logically, on
this basis, it should have been possible for *ne quis facere, fecisse,
velit* or *noli facere, fecisse* to denote 'No one should attempt—or,
dare—to do so and so', or 'Do not attempt—or, dare—to do
so and so'. I have found half an example only, a mock edict
posted up by Caesar's opponents to which I shall return.[5] But
this may be due to the casualness of my search or an accident
of transmission. (The request on a monument *ne quis velit obruere
cadaver*[6] employs the urbane form: 'Would no one, please, bury
a corpse here.' I have just quoted *noli me tangere* on a dead
person's lamp, clearly suppliant in tone; so is *noli violare* in an
epitaph, 'Would you, please, do no damage.'[7])

However, the interpretation of *ne quis fecisse velit* in early
official language as meaning 'No one should attempt—or,
dare—to do so and so' would not be satisfactory. True, something of the kind is universally accepted: the usual rendering is
'No one should be minded', half-way between 'attempt' and
'dare'. But for one thing, those sanctions of the type *si quis
facere vult* must be later than Cato. He argues that no law

---

[1] John 20. 17, in the Vulgate.   [2] C.I.L. I, no. 501.
[3] Bruns, 378, no. 9, 11 f.
[4] Bruns, 378, no. 3. The perfect infinitive in this clause need have no connexion
with the aorist, but may be put simply under the influence of the perfect tense of
voluerit.   [5] Suetonius, Caes. 80. 2; below, p. 48.
[6] Bruns, 382, no. 38. It does not seem to be early: *obruere* in the sense of 'to bury'
is generally regarded as post-Augustan.
[7] C.I.L. I, no. 1081; 6, no. 24752; earlier than the inscription cited in the last
footnote.

punishes a mere wicked desire, and that therefore no law ever inflicts a fine *si quis facere voluerit*.[1] Quite apart from this, it is *a priori* incredible that an ancient legislative form concentrated on attempt; and an emphasis on the presumptuous nature of the wrong would be somewhat academic. In any case, as already remarked, we must regard politeness, refinement, unwilling-ness to use a brutal imperative or jussive, as the normal object of the combination 'no one should wish' or 'do not wish' with a present infinitive. No bridge leads from this usage to the legislative *ne quis fecisse velit*.

I am inclined, therefore, to conclude that when the aoristic infinitive was continued and cultivated in official decrees, it was because of an element which distinguished it from the present, namely, the element of the past. *Ne quis fecisse velit*, that is, ought to be taken in the sense of 'No one should wish to have done so and so'—with a setting quite unlike that of *ne quis facere velit* or *noli facere*. Far from particularly urbane, it is particularly nasty. It contains a distinct threat. A man wishes to have done so and so—to have passed an examination which looms ahead, for example—if he imagines himself with pleasure in the situation that would be produced by the act. A warning not to wish to have done so and so implies that the situation would be anything but pleasurable. To wish for it would be most unwise. 'No one should wish to have acted in this way' signifies: if anyone does act in this way, he will rue it.

Presumably the form is influenced by the phraseology used in sentencing an offender:[2] *fecisse videtur*, 'he appears to have committed the crime', *corrupisse videtur*, 'he appears to have forged an official document', and so on. Here the perfect is entirely natural. The deed on which the tribunal pronounces is a matter of the past. (Just so the perfect is natural in the story of the patricians who were so proud of the murder of Gnaeus Genucius that even those that had taken no part 'wished to appear to have done it', 'to be deemed guilty', *fecisse videri vellent*.[3]) At the moment the prohibition is issued, the deed lies

---

[1] Gellius 6. 3. 37.   [2] Brissonius, *De Formulis*, ed. Conrad, 1731, 457.
[3] Livy 2. 54. 10.

in the future. But by putting the perfect in this peculiar fashion, 'No one should wish to have committed this or that crime', the lawgiver anticipates the time of the trial. He impresses on you how disagreeable it will be for you to find yourself in the position of one justly accused—hence avoid that position. He means: 'No one should wish to be found guilty of, to be sentenced for, this crime.'

In what connexion may this form have been found useful? The appearance of *ne* with the subjunctive excludes statutes proper. The most plausible answer is that the form was found useful by the senate or magistrates for exceptionally stringent prohibitions. We can, however, be more specific. One suspects that it originated where the senate or a magistrate, though refraining from setting forth the exact consequences of a transgression, yet wanted to let it be known that the decree could not be transgressed with impunity. This form threatens retaliation even though no special sanction is appended.

So far I have looked at the form as such, independently of the substance of any legislation where it occurs. This is the correct procedure from the point of view of form criticism. Let us now see whether the result accords with the evidence in general.

The form, though by no means frequent, is to be met with from very early down to the Augustan period. More precisely, it occurs in the edict by which the consuls fix the day for the centuriate assembly, prohibiting minor magistrates from watching the skies for unfavourable omens. According to Gellius,[1] the wording is *ex vetere forma perpetua*. We find it in the conditions of peace given to the Aetolians in 189 B.C.—but there is some doubt about the reading of the relevant clause,[2] 'Any of their dependencies which have recently come under Roman control they should not wish to have recovered', *ne recepisse velint*. It is prominent in the *senatusconsultum de Bacchanalibus* three years later. Livy, in his report, keeps this rare form,[3] an illustration of the tenacity of forms of which I spoke in the

---

[1] 13. 15. 1.   [2] Livy 38. 11. 9.
[3] 39. 14. 8; cp. Bruns, 165.

beginning. Further, it occurs in an edict issued by the consuls
on the same occasion in order to prevent the conspirators from
escaping. In this case it is only from Livy[1] that we may gather
that this form was employed. But the fact that he gives it is
conclusive. Again, the form reappears in a senatusconsult forbidding the dumping of rubbish in a certain region;[2] in an
edict of the praetor or, possibly, the aediles, which may well
have been initiated by the senate, and which forbids the
depositing of rubbish and corpses in urban districts;[3] in the
edict of the aediles forbidding the keeping of dangerous beasts
on a road commonly used;[4] in an inscription directed against
the alienation of a sepulchre;[5] and lastly, in a husband's order
to his wife in Terence,[6] and in Agamemnon's command to
leave Ajax unburied in Horace.[7]

The following points deserve notice. First, the form has its
seat in decrees by the senate and decrees by magistrates. Indeed,
it seems essentially to belong to the latter: the exceptions may
be only apparent. In Livy, one of the restrictions imposed
on the Aetolians is couched in this way. But he is not here
quoting the final treaty—characterized by the future imperative
—but the preliminary terms announced by the general in the
field;[8] or at least, he uses the style of these terms. The subjunctive is introduced in the previous sentence, where there is an
express reference to the consul's negotiations.[9] (Similarly, in
the *lex horrendi carminis* under which Horatius was tried,[10] the
first clause, with the subjunctive, *duumviri iudicent*, reflects the
appointment of the duumvirs, the rest, with future imperatives,
certato and so on, their instruction by the king or a statute.)
Polybius, who does not interrupt the final treaty by a reference
to the preliminary terms, has the imperative throughout.[11]
Again, the *senatusconsultum de Bacchanalibus* employs the form

---

[1] 39. 17. 3.   [2] Bruns, 189.   [3] Bruns, 190.   [4] Lenel, 566.
[5] Bruns, 379, no. 15.   [6] Hec. 563.   [7] Sat. 2. 3. 187.
[8] Cp. 38. 9. 10, with a simple *ne facerent*, however. Another example of preliminary terms in 34. 35. 1 ff.
[9] 38. 11. 8. The last term in 9, about the Oeniadae, switches back to the
imperative.   [10] Livy 1. 26. 6.
[11] 21. 32. 1 ff. In 21. 30. 1 ff., where the consul's preliminary agreement is given,
the infinitive is used.

discussed, yet exclusively in provisions which the senate recommends should be published by the magistrates as an edict. The senatusconsult protecting part of the *pagus Montanus* from rubbish probably also envisages the promulgation of an edict by the praetor or aediles.[1] The prohibition of the alienation of a sepulchre adopts edictal language. Terence achieves a comic effect by making a husband issue an interdict: *interdico ne extulisse puerum velis*, 'I caution you not to wish to have removed the child.' Note that this is not a general warning—*ne quis velit*—but one to a single person only. It is hardly accidental that where the husband speaks of a more general command to his slaves at large, he likens it to an edict: *edicam servis*, 'I will issue an ordinance to the slaves.' In Plautus[2] a procuress complains of her daughter's disregard for her interdicts—i.e. her orders not to yield to a certain admirer who is short of cash— and she charges the young lady with *imperium minuere*, 'lessening her *imperium*'. Horace's Agamemnon of course enjoys the highest magisterial power.

Secondly, the prohibitions showing this form are all particularly energetic: concerned with public order and decency, police measures, peace dictates to defeated enemies. As for the peace with the Aetolians, it may be recalled that they considered the condition respecting the dependencies to be excessively harsh and at first hesitated to accept it.[3] Moreover, in all cases a violation of the prohibition is heavily punished. It is certainly not advisable 'to have transgressed it'. This is true even of the first case—the consuls forbidding a watching of the skies—as to which Mommsen, with his accustomed intuition, remarked that a disobedient magistrate would 'naturally' be liable to a penalty.[4] It is obvious that an interpretation of the form as specially polite, like *noli facere*, would be misleading. We shall soon draw attention to other features confirming this, also to one or two which are incompatible with an interpretation of the form as referring to attempt or as stressing the presump-

[1] *Curarent arbitratu aedilium plebeium*, 'They should take care at the discretion of the aediles.'

[2] As. 504 ff.   [3] Livy 39. 9. 12, Polybius 21. 30. 8.

[4] *Staatsrecht*, vol. i, 3rd ed., 1887, 111 n. 1.

tuous nature of the offence, like *ne quis facere temptet* or *ne quis facere audeat*.

Thirdly, in most instances, certainly in the earlier ones, the punishment is indeterminate. I suggested above that the form, with its implied threat, 'it is inadvisable to have done so and so', must have had its primary setting in life where no explicit, detailed sanction was laid down.

The consular edict that 'no one should wish to have watched the skies' does not fix a penalty. Nor does the general tell the Aetolians exactly how he will proceed if they are recalcitrant. It is enough that he can be expected to react most drastically. (It makes little difference if the clause in question should be assigned to the final treaty: its breach would lead to heavy but indeterminate punishment, divine vengeance and a punitive expedition.) At first glance the *senatusconsultum de Bacchanalibus* contradicts the view here advanced: there is mention of capital punishment. But this portion does not belong to the edict which the senate asks the consuls to circulate. Whether we go as far as some scholars[1] who maintain that the passage is not concerned with future crimes at all but merely recounts how the senate dealt with what happened in the past, or whether we follow those[2] for whom it does set out the line the senate wishes to be taken in future—the actual edict recommended to the consuls begins after the words *ita edicendum censuere* and finishes before *haec ut edicatis*.[3] The mention of capital punishment lies outside it. Moreover, even those who regard the section as referring to future crimes admit that the senate's intention cannot possibly be to impose capital punishment for any contravention of its directions, serious or minor; it only authorizes this measure, without excluding less severe ones.[4] In other words, the section mentioning capital punishment, besides forming no part of the edict, leaves the penalty indeterminate. When we go on to the proclamation by the consuls that 'no one should wish to have sold or bought anything for

---

[1] E. Fraenkel, *Hermes* 67, 1932, 369 ff.; cp. Strachan-Davidson, *Roman Criminal Law*, vol. i, 1912, 232.
[2] Keil, *Hermes* 68, 1933, 306 ff.
[3] Bruns, 165, ll. 2, 23 at the beginning.   [4] Keil, 310 f.

the purpose of flight', we again find no sanction. There is one
in the senatusconsult forbidding the dumping of rubbish on
some ground; but the text is so fragmentary that we know
neither whether the sanction was very precise (the figure *HS*
in current editions is due to conjecture) nor whether it was
meant to be included in the edict which the senate apparently
envisaged. No sanction occurs in the praetorian edict forbidding
the depositing of rubbish or corpses in the city. It may be
added that Terence's husband and Horace's Agamemnon give
their orders without specifying the penalty in the event of
disobedience.

There remain only two cases with an accurately circumscribed sanction: the aedilician edict concerning dangerous
beasts and the prohibition of the alienation of a tomb. The latter
is here of small importance. The aedilician edict may have
begun without a sanction, to be provided with one later—
on the pattern of the praetorian edict *De his qui deiecerint.*[1] A
reminiscence of this development may be preserved in Paul's
Sententiae,[2] where the prohibition of keeping wild beasts by
the wayside is ascribed to the praetor, instead of the aediles. At
any rate, this edict is perhaps not very old.

Fourthly, no form corresponding to that here inspected
exists for positive commands. Neither in legal nor in lay sources
do we ever come across 'A man should wish to have done so
and so.' That this cannot be the result of chance, or of loss of
just those texts which contained such a command, is obvious
from the edict about the Bacchanals promulgated at the
recommendation of the senate. It begins: 'None of them should
wish to have had a Bacchanal.' Then it goes on to say that any
who think that they need a Bacchanal (because of a vow,
for example) 'should approach the praetor', *uti ad praetorem
venirent*. Here, where a positive command is laid down, it is
done by means of *ut* with the subjunctive, not by means of
'they should wish to have approached'.

Now if the prohibition 'No one should wish to have done so
and so' were specially civil, the absence of a corresponding

positive command would be inexplicable. It becomes natural
as soon as we realize that the prohibition is specially drastic,
that it alludes to the unpleasantness in store for you if you
disregard it. No corresponding pleasure awaits you if you observe
a positive command. It would be absurd to exhort you to look
forward with eagerness to the situation consequent on your
approach to the praetor—'They should wish to have approached
him.' Moreover, as we saw, the particular evil contemplated
by a prohibition 'No one should wish to have done so and so'
is the punishment you will suffer in case of contravention, or
rather, the sentence which will be delivered: *fecisse videtur*, 'he
appears to have committed the offence'. There is no analogous
traditional sentence for neglect of a positive command, no 'he
appears not to have fulfilled the order in question'. So the form
under discussion can have no parallel in the field of positive
commands; there can be only 'no one should wish to have done
this wrong'—a prohibition.

Fifthly, the form is used solely for the prohibition of acts,
never for the prohibition of qualities. It is used solely to tell you
'not to have done so and so', never to tell you 'not to have been
this or that'. Once again there is proof that the absence of
the latter application cannot be attributed to any gap in our
sources. In the *senatusconsultum de Bacchanalibus*, the warning
'not to have done so and so' occurs thirteen times. In fact it
is here the only form for the prohibition of acts. But when
it comes to a prohibition of a quality, of being this or that,
we find *sacerdos nequis vir esset*, 'no man may be a priest'.

The main explanation is that whereas it is normal for you to
wish to have performed an act which seems to lead to a desirable
result (to have passed an examination which will give you your
degree), so that you must be warned 'not to wish to have performed it' if the result is going to be undesirable ('do not wish
to have cheated in an examination'), you will never wish to
have possessed a desirable quality (to have been a fine man)
but to possess it and continue possessing it (to be a fine man).
Accordingly, if the quality is undesirable, you must be warned
'not to wish to be this or that' or rather—since this phrase is

unsuitable for legislation because of its role in polite speech—
'not to be this or that' ('do not be a conspirator'). But surely,
the language of judgments, too, is relevant. It is only in the
case of an act, which of necessity lies in the past, that a verdict
would be *fecisse videtur*, 'he appears to have done this'. In the
case of a quality, which ordinarily persists even at the moment
of the verdict, this would be *esse videtur*, 'he appears to be this
or that', e.g. 'the will produced seems to be forged'.[1] The
provision 'no one should wish to have performed secret rites'
refers forward to a possible sentence 'he appears to have performed secret rites'; the provision 'no man may be a priest' to
a sentence 'he appears to be a priest'.

This distinction, this limitation of 'No one should wish to
have offended' to acts, strongly supports the view that the form
involves a menacing allusion to condemnation in the event of
defiance. We can account for this distinction neither if we look
on the form as expressive of urbanity—for then, why should it
not extend to 'would no man, please, be a priest'?—nor if we
equate it with *ne quis facere temptet* or *audeat*, 'no one should try,
or dare, to do so and so', for in that case also there is no reason
why the lawgiver should avoid a clause like 'no man should try,
or dare, to be a priest'. By contrast, the distinction makes good
sense if we interpret the form as a threat: 'See that you will not
be in the position of one who has done so and so.' This perfect
will not do where a quality is to be proscribed. It might perhaps
be argued that *fuisse* lost its aoristic value earlier than the perfect infinitive of ordinary verbs, and that the absence of the
form from provisions directed against qualities ought to be
explained on this ground. But, not to mention other flaws,
there is a clause in the senatusconsult: *Neve affuisse vellent*,
'More than two men should not wish to have attended the rites.'[2]
If *affuisse* could be used in the sense of *adesse*—as according to
the hypothesis here combated it could be—it is difficult to
believe that *fuisse* could not be used in the sense of *esse*. The
truth is that *affuisse*, like the perfect infinitive of other verbs
occurring in the senatusconsult, must be understood as a perfect.

[1] Brissonius, loc. cit.   [2] Bruns, 165, ll. 20 f.

Participation in a ceremony is an act, not a quality. If a person commits this act, it will be said of him that 'he appears to have attended'. Hence the prohibition takes the form 'he should not wish to have attended'—attendance would be disastrous for him.

Sixthly, as is well known, Cato in his handbook on Agriculture imitates the style of legislation.[1] In the chapter giving the duties of an overseer, the form discussed is applied; and it is applied in a way exactly suiting our interpretation. It occurs only three times:[2] 'He should not wish to have bought anything without his master's knowledge, nor should he wish to have hidden anything from his master; he should not wish to have consulted fortune-tellers and astrologers,' *Nequid emisse velit, neve quid celavisse velit, Chaldaeum nequem consuluisse velit.* These are very serious warnings. They imply a threat in case of contravention, though the punishment is not strictly fixed. No parallels occur in positive commands (in the same section there is the injunction that 'he should settle his accounts with the master often', *putet*[3]) or in prohibitions of qualities as opposed to acts (*ne sit ambulator*, 'he should not be a gadabout', may also be found in the same section[4]). Cato shows a perfect knowledge of the function of this form.

Seventhly, it is to one of those naughty people who write on the walls of the places they visit (but Goethe did it too) that we owe the most direct corroboration of the thesis here advanced. 'No one should wish to have acted in such and such a way' might be paraphrased, I am suggesting, by 'If anyone does act in this way, he will be sorry for it'. It is in fact so paraphrased on a Roman boundary stone.

I have already referred to an edict of the praetor or aediles:[5] 'The praetor Sentius, in accordance with the senate's advice, has ordered that a district be marked off. No one should wish to have dumped rubbish or a corpse within the boundaries.' The edict is doubly preserved, i.e. on two stones. On one of them, however, there is a postscript, not engraved like the actual edict, but merely written: *Stercus longe aufer ne malum habeas,*

---

[1] Cp. below, pp. 94 ff.   [2] 5. 4.   [3] 5. 4   [4] 5. 2.   [5] Bruns, 190.

'Rubbish carry far off, or you will be in trouble.' Somebody substituted for the impersonal and negative provision of the edict a crude positive admonition directly addressed to any person who might come to this spot. But the spirit of the original, its character as a police measure and the menace which it implies, could not be rendered better; and, let us note again, it would never be the proper rendering of *noli me tangere* or *noli istum disturbare*.

We need not decide whether the prohibitive—or negative injunctive—*ne feceris* once implied a similar threat: 'May you not have done so and so', scil. and suffer for it. It would be surprising to find it in legislation. Originally it had regard to the immediate situation alone, 'do not hurt me', not to a general case, 'do not hurt a fellow-man'; in addition it was more or less confined to the second person. (This latter point is surely a corollary of the former: 'he should not do so and so' will normally refer to a general case and hardly ever to the immediate situation alone.) By the time it was applied with less discrimination, it had long ceased to imply a menace—if it ever did. Cato—as, following him, Columella[1]—employs *ne fecerit* in the sense of *ne faciat*: 'An overseer should lend oil to no one, *dederit nemini*; he may have two or three households to whom he lends, to no one besides, *quibus det, praeterea nemini*; he should not have, *ne habeat*, the same labourer for longer than a day.'[2] If he is copying legislation, it may be Oscan rather than Roman; in the *lex Osca tabulae Bantinae*[3] forms corresponding to *ne fecerit* and *ne fuerit* are common.

Why did the form *ne quis fecisse velit* die out about the end of the Republic? For one thing, its original import was lost sight of. A mock edict by Caesar's enemies runs:[4] 'No one should wish to show the House to any of these new senators', *ne quis monstrare velit*. This is hardly intended as polite, 'Would no one, please'. Much more likely it is intended as an imitation of those severe edicts with the form *ne quis fecisse velit*. But the perfect infinitive is replaced by the present, which renders the form empty. No wonder it was abandoned about that time.

[1] 1.8.5f.   [2] 5.3f.   [3] Bruns, 48 ff.   [4] Suetonius, *Caes.* 80. 2.

Two more factors may be mentioned. One, that important prohibitions leaving the punishment indeterminate had probably become rarer. The other, of a more general kind, that there is always a certain tendency for unusual forms, like *ne quis fecisse velit*, to be assimilated to the commoner ones, like *ne quis faciat*, even though this may involve the loss of some subtle nuance.

4. Headings and Operative Rules in Statutes

To proceed to a different topic; it may be useful to lay the ghost of a theory which has appeared on and off for close on a hundred years—namely, that a statute uses the imperative only in directions affecting magistrates without *imperium*, such as the quaestor, but refrains from using it towards those with *imperium*, such as the praetor. In the latter case, we are told, the less authoritative subjunctive is put. The doctrine goes back to Rudorff.[1] It was adopted by Ihering[2] and Karlowa.[3] And it is invoked by Wesenberg in a very recent treatise on the relation between the people and *magistratus maior* and on the latter's powers.[4] Certainly, if it were correct, far-reaching conclusions could be drawn. The application of two distinct forms to two kinds of magistrates would be of the greatest significance. It is, however, demonstrably false.

The first point to make one suspicious is that, according to Rudorff, the less authoritative subjunctive appears both in provisions concerning the praetor and in provisions concerning jurymen in a *quaestio*. The minor magistrates, then, to whom the statute gives instructions by means of an imperative are opposed to magistrates with *imperium* and jurors—a most unlikely division. It is interesting that Karlowa and Wesenberg make no mention of jurors—Ihering does still mention them—so that there is now a plausible contrast between magistrates with *imperium* and magistrates without. But Rudorff's evidence, such as it is, places the praetor and jurymen on the same level, both of them above the quaestor.

In the second place, Rudorff's observation refers solely to the

[1] *Ad legem Aciliam, Abhandlungen der Akademie der Wissenschaften zu Berlin*, 1861, 415.

[2] *Geist*, vol. ii, pt. 2, 6th and 7th ed., 1923, 604, n. 818. The remark must date at least from the 4th ed., 1858.

[3] *Römische Rechtsgeschichte*, vol. i, 1885, 462, n. 1.

[4] *Kontinuität zwischen königlicher Gewalt und Beamtengewalt, Savigny-Stiftung* 70, 1953, *Rom. Abt.*, 91.

lex Acilia, and Ihering still adheres to this limitation. Karlowa and Wesenberg represent it as a general feature of Roman statutes that they employ the imperative in dealing with minor magistrates, the subjunctive in dealing with those having *imperium.* Yet the only authority cited remains Rudorff.

In the third place, as far as the imperative in directions to minor magistrates is concerned, Rudorff relies on a single passage: *quaestor moram ne facito.*[1] Another, which is entirely reconstructed by him, *quaestor extra ordinem solvito,* and reconstructed differently by Mommsen, *quaestor ut solvat,* can hardly be said to count.[2] Again, as regards the subjunctive for the praetor and jurors, Rudorff admits an exception: *praetor rem agito.*[3] To be sure, this also is largely conjectural and unlike what we find in Mommsen.[4] But it provides a further indication of the precariousness of the whole theory.

The true position becomes clear as soon as we make a necessary distinction: between the operative part of a statute and the headings of its various sections. The rules belonging to the former are invariably couched in the imperative, whether they concern magistrates with *imperium,* magistrates without *imperium,* jurymen or anyone else. But with one apparent exception—which is the root of all the confusion—the imperative never occurs in a rubric.

The *lex Acilia,* on which Rudorff bases himself, lays down many duties of the praetor, all of them, if we disregard headings, in the imperative. *Praetor facito,* 'the praetor shall take steps to do so and so', is frequent.[5] But we also find the more direct *praetor iurato,* 'he shall take an oath',[6] *praetor quaerito,* 'he shall conduct the inquiry',[7] *praetor iubeto,* 'he shall order',[8] *praetor pronuntiato,* 'he shall pronounce the decision'.[9] As for jurors, the statute says *iudex manum demittito,* 'the juror shall put his hand in the box'.[10] Magistrates without *imperium* and civilians who are not jurymen are referred to in the imperative even according to

---

[1] Rudorff, 417; Bruns, 70, l. 69.
[2] Ibid.
[3] 416.
[4] Bruns, 66 f., ll. 49 f.
[5] E.g. 61, ll. 12, 15, 16.
[6] 61, l. 15, 62, l. 18.
[7] 64, l. 29.
[8] 64, l. 32.
[9] 66, ll. 42, 47.
[10] 67, l. 53.

the thesis here combated. We may list *qui petet in ius educito*, 'claimant shall bring his opponent into court',[1] *quaestor facito*[2]— obviously parallel to *praetor facito*—or *quaestor solvito*, 'he shall pay',[3] also *censor ne equum adimito*, 'the censor shall not take away his horse'.[4] The absence of any difference in form comes out very clearly in provisions like *qui praetor quaeret quive quaestor aerarium habebit facito*, 'the praetor or quaestor shall take steps to do so and so',[5] or *ne quis magistratus prove magistratu prove quo imperio potestateve erit facito neve iubeto*', 'no magistrate, promagistrate or other person exercising *imperium* or *potestas* shall take steps or order'.[6] This statute at least does not refrain from using the imperative in dealing with higher magistrates.

Neither does any other. The *lex Papiria de sacramentis* ordains: *praetor rogato*, 'the praetor shall propose'.[7] From the *tabula Bantina* we may quote: *praetor facito* (which occurs several times),[8] *quaestor facito*,[9] *praetor dato*, 'the praetor shall grant',[10] *magistratus quicumque comitia conciliumve habebit ne sinito*, 'no magistrate who holds a meeting of the whole people or of the *plebs* shall allow',[11] and *dictator, consul, praetor, magister equitum, censor, aedilis, tribunus plebis, quaestor, IIIvir capitalis, IIIvir agris dandis, iudex, iuranto*, 'a dictator, consul, praetor, master of the horse, censor, aedile, tribune, quaestor, officer for capital matters, officer for granting lands, judge, shall take an oath'.[12] The *lex Cornelia de XX quaestoribus* repeatedly says, *consules legunto*, 'the consuls shall choose',[13] and in exactly the same way, *quaestores legunto*.[14] These illustrations could be multiplied.

When, however, we look through the chapter headings in statutes, the result is just the reverse. No matter what kind of magistrate is referred to, and even if no magistrate is referred

---

[1] Bruns, 62, l. 19.   [2] 69, l. 68.

[3] 69, l. 64, 70, l. 69.

[4] 64, l. 28. The word *censor* is not extant and not supplied by Bruns, but it is plainly the right word; see e.g. Hardy, *Roman Laws and Charters*, 1912, 19.

[5] 70 f., ll. 72 f. Cp. *neve quis iudex* (which term here denotes the praetor) *neve quaestor facito*, 68, l. 61.   [6] 70, l. 70.

[7] 47.   [8] E.g. 54, ll. 10, 11.

[9] 55, l. 21.   [10] 54, ll. 9 f.

[11] 53, l. 6.   [12] 54, ll. 15 f.

[13] 89 f., ll. 7 f., 90, ll. 11 f., 16 f.   [14] 91, ll. 8 f., 12 f.

to at all, the imperative is strictly avoided. As already remarked, there is one apparent exception, which I shall discuss presently. For the moment, here are a number of typical rubrics of the *lex Acilia*: *De CDL viris legundis*, 'On 450 men to be elected'[1]—this election is the duty of the praetor—*Quos legerit eos indicet*, 'Of those whom he (the praetor) chooses he should indicate particulars',[2] *Praetor ut interroget*, 'The praetor should interrogate',[3] *Eidem iudices sint*, 'The same jurors should remain throughout the case',[4] *Iudex nequis disputet*, 'No juror should interrupt',[5] *De reis quomodo iudicetur*, 'How a verdict should be given'[6]—this involves duties of the praetor and the jurors—*Reliquum in aerario sit*, 'The residue should remain in the treasury'[7]—this concerns duties of the quaestor, without *imperium*—*Pecunia obsignetur*, 'The money should be sealed up'[8]—scil. by the quaestor—*De nomine deferundo*, 'On the summons to be registered'[9]—this must be done by claimant, who may be an ordinary civilian and, indeed, an alien.

Rudorff rests his theory on such clauses as *Praetor ut interroget* and *Iudex nequis disputet*, with the subjunctive for praetor and juryman. But they confirm only that the imperative does not figure in rubrics. It does not figure there even if neither a praetor nor a juryman is involved.

Before going into the one case which at first sight fails to conform to the rule, let me put the question all-important from the form critical point of view: why is the imperative confined to the principal part of a statute and excluded from its titles? The answer is that it is only in the principal part of a statute that the people actually commands, exercising its sovereignty. The titles are added for the sake of convenience, of a better arrangement and understanding of the contents. They merely give a clue to the topic and object of the following section. In brief statutes none appear at all. They are not commands.

Quite possibly, when a *lex rogata* is proposed to the assembly,

[1] Bruns, 61, ll. 12, 15.
[2] 61, l. 14, 62, l. 17.
[3] 65, l. 35.
[4] 64, l. 27.
[5] 65, l. 39.
[6] 66, l. 49.
[7] 69, l. 64.
[8] 69, l. 67.
[9] 62, l. 19.

the headings are not even mentioned. It is difficult to see how the question *velitis iubeatis*, 'would you wish and order' (whether followed by a final *ut* or by an accusative and infinitive[1]) could be separated from the operative injunctions by a rubric or rubrics—especially when we remember that a rubric might, for example, take the form of a *quomodo* sentence: *Iudices in consilium quomodo eant*, 'How jurors should deliberate'.[2] But even in a *lex data*, the headings are manifestly not intended as binding. Otherwise a heading like *De obligatione praedum*, 'Concerning the obligation of sureties'—in the *lex Malacitana*[3]—would make no sense.

I now come to the difficulty created by a passage in the *lex Acilia* which looks like a heading with an imperative: *Quaestor moram ne facito*, 'The quaestor shall cause no hindrance'.[4] From the foregoing considerations it is certain that, whatever the explanation may be, it cannot be that the statute means to discriminate between the quaestor on the one hand and the praetor, or the praetor and jurymen, on the other. I submit that this sentence is not a heading at all. If, on the plate, it is given as a heading, this is due to an error of the cutter. An imperative in a heading would be not only unique but also absurd.

It is relevant to note that, only two lines farther on,[5] the inscriber forgot about a heading he ought to have put, *Iudex deinceps faciat*, 'The successor should take steps'[6]—a slip which made it necessary for him, after another seven lines, to re-write

[1] Mommsen, *Staatsrecht*, vol. iii, pt. 1, 312, n. 2, regards *ut* as regular. (That he means a final *ut*, not *uti vos rogo*, 'as I ask you', is clear, for one thing, from the dots between *uti* and *vos rogo*, and for another, from the fact that his first text, Gellius 5. 19. 9, has *ut* with the subjunctive leading up to *vos rogo*.) Of the passages he adduces, quite a few do not purport to contain a direct quotation of the magistrate's question: Cicero, Verr. 2. 2. 67, with *ut*, Livy 1. 46. 1, 21. 17. 4, 30. 43. 2, 31. 6. 1, 36. 1. 5 and 45. 21. 4 (this last-mentioned misprinted 44. 21. 4), with the accusative and infinitive. We find direct quotations with *ut* in Livy 38. 54. 3, Cicero, De domo 17. 44, Pis. 29. 72, Gellius 5. 19. 9, with the accusative and infinitive in Livy 22. 10. 2. The latter construction looks nicer. It is arguable, however, that *ut* is the genuine thing, since a writer would more readily have given it up in favour of the accusative and infinitive than the other way round.

[2] Bruns, 66, l. 46.   [3] 153.

[4] 70, l. 69.   [5] 70, l. 72.

[6] It seems to me, incidentally, that contrary to the prevalent view of editors, *faciat* in this rubric was not used absolutely, but something like (*ut*) *omnia fiant* followed: 'The successor should take steps that all may be done'.

this fairly long portion of the law with the heading originally omitted.[1] An engraver who carelessly leaves out a rubric is not above carelessly making a rubric of a substantive provision. Very speculatively, we may even connect his two mistakes. He was told the number of sections to be marked off from each other by headings; since he wrongly treated *quaestor moram ne facito* as a heading, he wrongly neglected to insert a real heading, *Iudex deinceps faciat;* he thus kept to the right number; and it was only at some later stage of the work that a supervisor discovered the oversight and required the addition of the missing title.

In any case, *quaestor moram ne facito* is no rubric. Two further points may be noted in this connexion. First, of the following sentence, only the letter *q* is preserved, generally taken to be the first letter of *quaestor*. This may be correct. But once we realize that there is here no heading, a relative pronoun or conjunction such as *qui, quod, quominus*, is just as likely.[2] (On the other hand, it is arguable that the cutter assumed a heading precisely because the following sentence again began with *quaestor*.) Secondly, the statute contains the words *is praetor ei moram ne facito*[3] which are not written as a heading. They are definitely an actual command, and so is *quaestor moram ne facito*.

Here may be the place to comment on an inaccurate restoration of a line of the *lex Acilia*, which could have been avoided by paying closer attention to forms. All editors are agreed that line 25 contains a rule according to which, if a person prefers a claim and the defendant fails to make use of his right to select and name fifty jurors, *tum ei per eum praetorem adversariumve mora non erit quominus legat edatve*, 'then he (plaintiff) will suffer no hindrance by the praetor or his opponent from selecting and naming them'.[4] But quite apart from the queer and complicated negative expression, 'he will suffer no hindrance from selecting', where a positive one would do, 'he will select', this use

---

[1] See Bruns, 70 f., nn. 2 f., 73, n. 1.

[2] As for *quominus* after *mora*, cp. two passages in the same statute, 63, l. 25, and 65, l. 35, and a resolution of the senate, 190.

[3] 65, l. 35.

[4] E.g. Rudorff, 452, 540, Bruns, 63, l. 25.

of the future instead of the imperative is impossible in a statute. *Mora non erit*, 'there will be no hindrance', cannot replace *mora ne esto*, 'there shall be no hindrance'. It should be observed that the *lex Acilia* twice declares *actio ne esto*.[1]

Now of this alleged rule with the future, the words *tum ei* at the opening are due to mere conjecture. Of *erit*, only the letter *e* seems assured.[2] And after *edatve* at the end there is a lengthy gap which we must fill in as best we can. There is, then, no evidence whatever that we have before us a principal clause—stating a prohibition by means of the future—while from a consideration of the form it emerges that it must be a subordinate one.

Exactly how the original ran, we cannot say. But *cui* or *si ei* or *si* is far preferable to *tum ei*. On this basis, the person designated by the pronoun may well be not the plaintiff, but the defendant. The rule is probably to the effect that if a man prefers a claim and the defendant fails to make use of his right to select and name fifty jurors, 'provided he (defendant) suffers no hindrance by the praetor or his opponent from selecting and naming them', that is to say, provided his inaction is not the fault of the magistrate or plaintiff, the right shall pass to the latter. This allows us to read *mora non est* or *mora non erit*.[3] It explains the negative expression, 'provided the hindrance is not (will not be) by the praetor or opponent'; a positive expression would not do. As for the imperative ordaining that, given the necessary conditions, plaintiff may name the jurors instead of defendant, this must be in the long gap which follows *edatve*.

---

[1] Bruns, 67, l. 56, 71, ll. 75, 82. The negation of the imperative is always by means of *ne*, so that the reading *mora non esto* is precluded.

[2] It appears as *e[rit...]* in Rudorff, 452, as *eri[t...]* in Rudorff, 540, as *er[it...]* in Bruns. The inscription, by the way, shows *morm*, not *mora*, but the lawgiver doubtless intended the latter.

[3] In l. 11 of the statute (Bruns, 60) 'he whose client defendant will be', *erit*, is excluded from being a patron, in l. 33 (Bruns, 65) 'he who is defendant's client', *sit*, is excluded from giving evidence.

5. Change of Grammatical Subject

In conclusion, a remark on the use of the third person singular in the XII Tables. We cannot, indeed, here speak of a form of legislation, since the point is a general, grammatical one, affecting lay literature as well. But the matter is much misunderstood, yet essential to a proper assessment of the milieu of the codification and, more particularly, of the degree of synthesis of thought still prevalent at this epoch.

What is regularly overlooked is the fact that, in ancient Latin, the so-called third person singular may have an impersonal sense. As a result of this wrong start, scholars are driven to build up strange theories—such as that ancient authors had a liking for a change of grammatical subject. However, in the XII Tables, in most cases where the prevalent view assumes a change of subject, we have more probably to do with the impersonal form.

Voigt[1] and Karlowa[2] claim that in the short section from *Si in ius vocat* to *iacito*,[3] the subject changes five times: 'If he (plaintiff) summons to court, he (defendant) shall go; if he (defendant) does not go, he (plaintiff) shall call witnesses; thereupon he (plaintiff) shall take him (defendant); if he (defendant) devises tricks or flees, he (plaintiff) shall arrest him (defendant).' But the correct translation (accepting *ito* as part of the law which, as we have seen,[4] it certainly was not) seems to be: 'If there is summoning, there shall be going; if there is no going, there shall be calling of witnesses; thereupon one shall take him (defendant); if there is devising of tricks or fleeing, there shall be arresting of him (defendant).'

At this stage of the language, whereas *amo* and *amas* indicate exactly the person performing the action, 'I love', 'you love', *amat*, unless a subject is named, as a rule simply means that

---

[1] *Die XII Tafeln*, vol. i, 1883, 89.
[2] *Römische Rechtsgeschichte*, vol. i, 1885, 115.
[3] Bruns, 17 f.   [4] Above, pp. 28 f.

someone is performing it. It describes the occurrence as a whole, without pointing out the person—except that it would not be the first or second.[1] It is not yet specialized to the extent to which it is, say, two hundred years later. We are sometimes told—I do not know how true it is—that the primitives count 'one, two, many'. In ancient Latin, the persons are, roughly speaking, 'I love, you love, one loves'. The imperatives *amato* and *amamino* are even more general. They express a command to the second person, to the third person, or indefinite. In the XII Tables, it is usually the latter. The beautifully logical Alexandrian system, with its clear-cut first person, second person, third person, is still a long way off; not to mention the fact that it never truly reflected the reality of a living language.

I refrain from seeking support in the origins of the endings designating the third person, since they are highly controversial; though it seems to me that all theories about them advanced so far suit the view I am proposing. However, I would draw your attention to these suggestive points.

In the first place, there are languages, like German, where constructions analogous to 'it rains' still cover a much wider range than in English: *es brennt, es telephoniert* and so forth. Actually, in colloquial speech, it would be quite in order to say, for *si in ius vocat*: *Wenn es zu Gericht ruft.*

In the second place, there was a time when the verbs now classed as impersonal were far from constituting a strictly separate group. They were not confined to that use at all. Ζεὺς ὕει is at least as old as ὕει; *libet*, 'it pleases', is impersonal in classical Latin, but Plautus says *quo lubeant nubant*, 'let them marry whom they please'.[2] It is clear that these verbs only became impersonal in the full sense by the other use dying out. Similarly, in the case of the majority of verbs, it is the impersonal use which died out, the form *amat* acquiring the specialized role of third person. But the XII Tables lie before this evolution.

---

[1] Of course, you may deliberately provide with an impersonal dress a statement in reality having regard to the first or second person. The poor fellow in Plautus, Pseud. 1. 3. 45. 273, who says *amatur atque egetur*, 'one loves and cannot afford it', means himself. The humour of the passage consists precisely in his avoiding the first person.   [2] Aul. 3. 5. 17. 491.

In the third place, it is relevant to note that *amat* became specialized later than *amo* and *amas* not only in the matter of person, but also in that of number. Originally it includes both the singular and plural. It is true that it no longer does so in the XII Tables—though the impersonal use in a way covers both numbers—but in Greek, for instance, a distinct trace remains in the rule that if the third person of a verb refers to a neuter subject, it must be in the singular whether the subject is in the singular or plural. This rule has been found most perplexing,[1] but there is little difficulty if we see in it a survival of the very comprehensive scope of *amat*. Previous explanations— such as that the plural of neuter subjects often denoted a collective—are not quite adequate. They do not account for the fact that the rule applies only if the verb is in the third person, but not if it is in the first or second. They may still be useful in showing why, when *amat* was replaced by *amant* where connected with a masculine or feminine plural, it was not replaced where connected with a collective, a neuter plural. But we must assume an earlier stage at which, while the first and second persons possessed a singular and plural, *amat* did for both numbers.[2] Cicero, in his De Legibus, says that two supreme magistrates *consules appellamino*, 'shall be called consuls'.[3] This use of the imperative in -*mino* for the plural, not attested anywhere else, is regarded by Stolz-Schmalz as 'an ill-formed archaism' (*ein missratener Archaismus*).[4] Perhaps the critics are right. But though it would be surprising to find an early text employing the imperative in just this kind of sentence—subject ('the magistrates'), imperative in -*mino* ('shall be called'), completion of the predicate ('consuls')—Cicero may well have known, say, a

---

[1] See Blass, *Grammatik des neutestamentlichen Griechisch*, 5th ed. by Debrunner, 1921, 81: *Wohl keine syntaktische Eigentümlichkeit des Griechischen ist uns auffälliger.*

[2] In speaking of a plural of the first person, I am adopting the established terminology. But, obviously, whereas it is reasonable to call *vos* the plural of *tu*— since *tu* and *tu* make *vos*—and *isti* the plural of *iste*—since *iste* and *iste* make *isti*—it is at least ambiguous to call *nos* the plural of *ego*. It is not *ego* and *ego* that make *nos*, but *ego* and *tu* or *ego* and *iste*. Another illustration of the elegance of the Alexandrian scheme blurring important distinctions.

[3] 3. 3. 8.

[4] *Lateinische Grammatik*, 5th ed. by Leumann and Hofmann, 1928, 308.

law where *famino* meant 'there shall be saying' in the sense of 'they, i.e. several parties, shall say'.

By the time of Lucilius, however, it was already possible, for the purpose of a pleasantry at least, to treat those verbs of the old codification as in the third person. He writes:[1] *Si non it capito, inquit, eum et si calvitur. Ergo fur dominum?*, 'If he does not go, the law says, he shall take him, also if he devises tricks. So the thief is to take the owner?'

Maybe this idea is even older. Somebody in Plautus observes of thievish cooks that wherever they are, *duplici damno dominos multant*, 'they exact a twofold penalty from their masters'.[2] In other words, instead of the owners fining the thieves, these thieves fine the owners. The joke can no doubt stand on its own feet. But, very possibly, underlying it was a traditional one about the 'change of subject' in the provision of the XII Tables:[3] *Si adorat furto, duplione damnum decidito*, 'If he (plaintiff) brings a charge of theft, he (defendant) shall pay a twofold penalty'. It may have been a current jest to refer the second half also to plaintiff. The original meaning is: 'If there is a charge of theft, there shall be a coming to terms as to the penalty by means of twofold restitution.'

Another feature now becomes explicable and, indeed, corroborates what I am saying about the early scope of the so-called third person. The XII Tables put *si*, 'if', where later statutes put *si quis*, 'if anybody'. This is usually noted as a mere oddity, an irrational archaism.[4] But it is not that. Certainly, as soon as we render *amat* as 'loves', we do require a specific subject, express or implied. We must then translate *si in ius vocat* by 'if summons'; which necessarily leads to the question 'who summons?', with the reply 'anybody', *aliquis*. The absence of *quis* from the code will appear unjustifiable; it will leave a gap; the clause will not construe properly. In point of fact, however, *amat* primarily signifies 'there is loving', 'one loves'. Accordingly, *si in ius vocat* should be translated by 'if there is summoning',

---

[1] Nonius 7. 1 ff.
[2] Casina 3. 6. 3. 722. See Daube, *Studi Solazzi*, 1948, 97.
[3] Bruns, 33—somewhat conjectural.
[4] Karlowa, loc. cit.

si membrum rupsit by 'if there has been breaking of a limb' and so on. No *quis* is missing. The clauses in question are quite complete and logical. When later statutes put *si quis*, it is because, by that time, *amat* has indeed become the third person proper.

Remember, however, that even so its former function is carried on both by the so-called third person plural, *amant*, *vocant*, 'they love', 'they summon', in the indefinite sense of 'one loves', 'one summons'—*aiunt*, 'they say', is a familiar case—and by the so-called third person singular of the passive, *amatur*, *vocatur*. *Amatur atque egetur*, 'one loves and cannot afford it', says the playwright,[1] and, less gloomily, *bibitur estur*, 'there is feasting and drinking'.[2] We need not here inquire why the plural and the passive remained less specialized; like Coningsby, we have already lived long enough to know that it is not wise to wish everything explained. The point is that, just as we do not think of supplying *aliqui* or *aliquid* where *amant* or *amatur* is used impersonally, so, in the XII Tables, we ought not to supply anything where *amat* is used in this sense. To do so means imposing on ancient speech our modern—or rather, the Alexandrian—grammatical categories, instead of interpreting it in accordance with the syntax of the time.

[1] Plautus, Pseud. 1. 3. 45. 273; see above, p. 58, n. 1.
[2] Poen. 4. 2. 13. 835.

II

1. Ethical Rules

DEAN SWIFT has remarked: 'The Society of writers would quickly be reduced to a very inconsiderable number if men were put upon making books with the fatal confinement of delivering nothing but what is to the purpose.' My talk is going to illustrate the truth of his observation. For I wish to begin by looking at a few forms not strictly belonging to legislation, though perhaps near enough to be of interest; and first of all, at the way in which ethical rules were expressed in Rome.

What strikes one most in this field is the complete absence of anything resembling the authoritative injunctions so common in the Old Testament. Take three maxims quoted by Cicero as well established:[1] 'One should not deny others the use of one's stream; one should allow others to take fire from one's fire, if anybody wishes for this; one should give honest counsel to him who deliberates', *Non prohibere aqua profluente; pati ab igne ignem capere, si qui velit; consilium fidele deliberanti dare.* What a contrast, from the point of view of form, to, say, 'Thou shalt not avenge, nor bear any grudge against the children of thy people, but thou shalt love thy neighbour as thyself; I am the Lord.'[2] Note, in the Latin, the didactic infinitive, taking the place of a proper imperative. Note the lame *si qui velit*, 'allow the taking of fire from your fire—if anyone wishes for it'. Note also the governing principle which, according to Cicero, underlies these and many similar precepts: 'For such conduct is useful to the recipient and not troublesome for the giver.'

Manifestly, these Roman ethical rules are pieces of good advice based on experience rather than absolute eternal commands; and essentially the closest parallels in the Bible occur in the Wisdom Literature, i.e. in the Proverbs, Ecclesiastes

[1] Off. 1. 16. 52.   [2] Lev. 19. 18.

and the like. I say 'essentially the closest', meaning that it is in the Proverbs, Ecclesiastes and the like that we find a morality which, whatever its detailed demands, breathes this spirit of worthy and slightly pedantic utilitarianism. On the other hand, it is superficial to think that where one of those categorical injunctions of the Bible ordains the same as a quiet infinitive of Cicero, we have before us the same kind of ethics. Certainly, *consilium fidele deliberanti dare* in a way corresponds to 'Thou shalt not curse the deaf, nor put a stumblingblock before the blind, but thou shalt fear thy God; I am the Lord.'[1] But there is a profound difference: the Roman precept is Wisdom, instruction, conservative, the Biblical the Will of God, adjuration, revolutionary. This is not to deny that there is great depth and strength in 'Wisdom morality'; but the distinction between it and 'prophetic morality' is a real one. There are many cases like that quoted where the use of form critical methods could prevent a hasty assumption or overrating of parallels. Though two rules are similar in substance, yet a consideration of form may show them to go back to very dissimilar milieus.

The worldly character of Roman ethical precepts remains noticeable even where proper imperatives or jussives are put, and not, as in the passage from Cicero just discussed, infinitives. A decent person, Lucilius holds,[2] *curet aegrotum, sumptum homini praebeat, genium suum defraudet, ali parcat*, 'should look after one who is sick, should pay the man his expenses, should deny himself, should spare the other'. Here the subjunctive is used; but still the style is prosaic and dry, not at all reminiscent of the passionate commandments of the Bible. The point comes out well in Terence's Adelphi,[3] where a strict father boasts that he misses no opportunity of informing his son of moral precepts; and that he keeps telling him *Hoc facito, hoc fugito*, 'This do, that avoid'. It is quite plain that these imperatives are of an advisory force only, for the old man goes on describing how he preaches: *Hoc laudist, hoc vitio datur*, 'This is creditable, that is reckoned a fault'. He is explaining to his son what the world thinks of

[1] Lev. 19. 14. [2] Non. 117. 24.
[3] 3. 3. 417 f.

various actions. We are again moving in the sphere of Wisdom; and, significantly, the slave to whom the father is talking, flatters him by saying: *Nil nisi sapientia es*, 'You are Wisdom incarnate.'[1]

Actually, this slave permits himself a parody on the father's sermonizing.[2] He says that he schools his undercooks in exactly the way in which the father schools his son. He tells them, for instance: 'This is too salt, that is burned; this is insufficiently cleaned, that is right—remember to do it like this again.' To transfer to the kitchen the solemn tone of moral instruction is, of course, ridiculous. But the fact is that, at Rome, no great change in form is needed to effect this transfer. It is precisely this near-ness of one domain to the other which enables the slave to draw his cheeky comparison, to which the old man, though greatly annoyed, is powerless to reply. When King James's cook speaks Latin to his colleagues,[3] the joke is of a different kind. It is based, not on the nearness, but on the extreme distance between the scholarly circles at the Court and the servants' hall; and there is no room for any cheeky assimilation.

It is no exaggeration to assert that the forms employed by the Romans for ethical rules are identical with those to be found in any other didactic branch of literature—such as Cato's and Varro's works on Agriculture or Ovid's Art of Love.

[1] 3. 3. 394.
[2] 3. 3. 423 ff.
[3] Scott, Fortunes of Nigel 2. 14.

2. Infinitive

A few words may be said about the imperatival infinitive we have just come across in Cicero: *non prohibere aqua profluente*, 'one should not deny the use of one's stream'. To go by Stolz-Schmalz,[1] in literary Latin, this usage does not antedate Valerius Flaccus,[2] though in the vernacular it is much earlier. Presumably, according to Stolz-Schmalz, either the maxims quoted by Cicero are of popular origin, or we ought to regard them as dependent on *sunt illa communia* and translate: 'There are those principles not to deny the use of a stream, to allow others to take fire, to give honest counsel.' Similar infinitives may indeed be found in Cato and Varro, for instance: *Infervescito paulisper, postea iusculum sorbere et brassicam esse*, 'Boil for a short time, afterwards one should drink the broth and eat the cabbage.'[3] But here, in the opinion of Stolz-Schmalz, we ought to supply a verb like *debes* and render: 'Afterwards you must drink the broth.'

This view, however, is not convincing. We must distinguish between an admonition having regard to a specific situation—of the type 'Come in'—and one of a general character—of the type 'Always tell the truth'. It may be admitted that, in literary Latin, the infinitive does not stand for the former type before Valerius Flaccus, who writes: *tu socios adhibere sacris*, 'do you summon your comrades to the sacrifice'. The action is to be performed on this occasion only, and only by a definite person: note the mention of *tu*, 'you do so and so'. But the infinitive does stand for the latter type at least from Cato onwards. There is absolutely no reason why we should supply a verb like *debes* in the passages concerned.

What, then, is the setting in life of this infinitive which serves as a general admonition? The present infinitive (and it is only the present infinitive which is employed in this manner) ex-

[1] 590 f.
[2] 3. 412.
[3] Cato, R.R. 156. 7.

presses the verbal notion as such, in its purity. We should expect
to find it where the main purpose is simply to draw attention to
the notion in question. Thus it occurs in some of Cato's headings—this is conceded by Stolz-Schmalz—such as *Odorem deterio-
rem demere vino*, 'To remove bad odour from wine'.[1] The same
purpose, however, would lead to its use in a quiet, sober plan,
to describe a step or series of steps to be taken. The fact that the
steps are necessary is sufficiently indicated by their appearing
in a plan. Hence an author who writes an unemotional, matter-
of-fact style may dispense with a proper imperative or jussive;
he may be satisfied with the infinitive, a mere reminder of the
action called for. 'Attend Faculty meeting Tuesday, see Olga
Sunday' would be possible entries in a diary (though, in English,
the gerund is often preferred: 'Monday—washing, Thursday—
painting'). Similarly, Cato says: *Infervescito, postea sorbere et esse*,
'Boil, then (to) drink the broth and (to) eat the cabbage.'
Drinking the both and eating the cabbage are ordinary, un-
exciting parts of the scheme recommended. In these pedestrian
directions the imperatival infinitive is perfectly appropriate.

Nor is it surprising to meet with it in Roman ethical maxims.
We have already seen that they are not at bottom very different
from other pieces of practical advice. *Non prohibere aqua profluente, consilium fidele deliberanti dare*—these are items of a pro-
gramme, of a rather dull outline of decent living.

By contrast, there is no room for this infinitive in legislation,
be it statutes or magisterial decrees. Legislation intends to do
more than calmly point out a course, it intends to compel you
to that course. It is remarkable that in this field the infinitive
never figures even in headings. (I am not counting such cases
as *iudicatum solvi*,[2] which represents *cautio*, or *de cautione, iudicatum
solvi*.) For one thing, it is not dignified, formal enough. *De* with
the gerund—*de in ius vocando, de edendo*[3]—is more suitable for the
Edict. But part of the explanation surely lies in the lawgiver
being less of a detached guide and more of a ruler with an
interest in being obeyed. Even in a heading, therefore, when a

---

[1] 110. [2] Lenel, 530.
[3] Lenel, 65, 59.

desirable or undesirable action is to be named, he will incline to avail himself of a subjunctive—with or without *ut* or *ne*—or a gerundive construction. *Pecunia in fiscis obsignetur, praetor ut interroget, de nomine deferendo*, are titles in the *lex Acilia*,[1] *ne quis vi eximat, de loco publico fruendo*, in the Edict.[2] This is not to deny that the rubrics of a didactic work may be composed in the same way. The point here to be made is that the imperatival infinitive is quite absent from legislation.

[1] Bruns, 69, 65, 62. [2] Lenel, 73, 459.

3. Present Indicative

LET us go on to consider another remarkable form shown by many extra-legal precepts—rules of sound management, etiquette, ethics, religion—though never by any legal ones: the simple indicative, more precisely, the third person of the present indicative. We find quite a few examples in the list of rules for the priests of Jupiter, which I have already mentioned: 'A priest of Jupiter has a knot in his head-dress; he does not pass under slips shooting forth beyond the ordinary height from vines.'[1] The nearest equivalent, if we wanted a fuller expression of the binding nature of these directions, would be: 'It is customary, *mos est*, for a priest of Jupiter to have a knot in his head-dress; it is not done for him to pass under slips shooting forth from vines.' We may recall that it is *mos est* and similar phrases (*oportet, religio est* and so on) that dominate this list.

The question here to be put is: What is the social background, the setting in life, of rules employing the simple indicative? In what circumstances would there be a real point in preferring 'A priest has a knot in his head-dress' to 'It is proper, customary, for a priest to have a knot'? The Concise Oxford Dictionary says of the indicative that it presents 'a thing as a fact, not as conception, wish etc., of speaker'.[2] Our question may, then, be restated thus: What would be the purpose of introducing a precept as an existing fact—as a present indicative?

There would be a negative and a positive purpose. The former would be to exclude certain ideas connected with such forms of precepts as the imperative, the jussive, *oportet, mos est*: the ideas of constraint and authority. The indicative is put to emphasize that there is no occasion either for constraint or for reliance on an authority. The addressees of these rules need not be ordered to do this and refrain from that. They need not even be impressed by the mention of any ultimate power like religion

---

[1] Gellius 10. 5. 9, 13.   [2] New ed., 1929, 580.

or tradition. At most they may have to be informed of the right actions—which they automatically do once they know them. A priest of Jupiter—as far as his rules are couched in this form—is assumed to conduct himself in a certain mode, not under compulsion or from obedience, but as a matter of course.

Yet there is a positive purpose also. 'A priest has a knot', though avoiding constraint and invocation of authority, is more forceful than, say, the present infinitive—'to eat this, to drink that'—or the polite *noli me tangere*. The greater force lies in the implication that, where you do not find the action or quality, the predicate, in question, by definition you cannot have to do with the person or thing, the subject, in question. 'A priest has a knot' implies that a man without such a knot is not a priest, at any rate, not a proper, ideal one; the presupposition being that he would like to be one. In this way, a rule using the present indicative carries a sanction within itself: it is, so to speak, a *lex perfectissima*.

It follows that this form, the present indicative, is particularly suitable for rules to be observed by select bodies, the members of which are—or are supposed to be—proud of living differently from the multitude, proud of possessing a distinctive code. It is in laying down directions for such groups that this appeal to pride is natural and, indeed, of the most immediate usefulness. To remind people that the *élite* among which they are counted does certain things and eschews others, and to insinuate that they would not be counted among it if they did not follow these practices, can be far more effective than direct commands, references to authority, detached counsels or courteous requests. It should also be noted that it is by means of the indicative that the outside world will be told of, and will itself talk and write about, the ways of the chosen. 'The Pharisees', Josephus reports,[1] 'think little of the pleasures of life; they pay homage to those advanced in age. The Essenes neither marry nor keep slaves.' This is a description by an outsider, and for outsiders, of the life of two sects. But as far as form is concerned, it might as well be the rules agreed on by 'those within'.

[1] Ant. 18. 3. 12 ff.

The interpretation of these precepts as given for the chosen is true not only of Rome, but quite generally, down to this day. If the priests of Jupiter were a company finding the form service-able, so are the Scouts: paragraph 2 of the Scout Law begins 'A Scout is loyal to the King', paragraph 4 'A Scout is a friend to all'. But even if I tell my son 'A decent boy gets up when a lady is looking for a seat in a bus', there is still a trace of the original function of the form: I am suggesting to him that he belongs to a special band—the band of decent boys.

In numerous cases the form under discussion is much attenu-ated. Varro writes:[1] 'Freshly clipped sheep they rub down; sheep with coarse fleece they shear about harvesting time.' That this is mainly didactic description of the proper, usual procedure may be seen from the continuation: 'Some shear their sheep twice a year.' None the less we may detect a slight adumbration of the idea that good farmers rub down clipped sheep, and that if you do not do it you are not a good farmer. A little farther on, in the same section, we are told: 'The more careful are accustomed to shear their sheep over cloths in order that no wool may be lost.' According to Virgil,[2] if bad weather prevents work out of doors, 'the ploughman mends the blunted share, sets a brand on his flocks' and so on. Again, while the prevalent tone is that of instruction, there is a hint that one who passes such periods in laziness is not a farmer in the true sense of the word.

The setting in life indicated explains also why this form never occurs in legislation proper (by which I mean here any laws emanating from the state, whether statutes, senatusconsults or edicts). Legislation proper, even where it is concerned—as on occasion it may be—with a picked section of the nation only, does not rely on the appeal to pride. It would be out of keeping with the very essence of legislation to stress the voluntary, matter-of-course nature of the conduct desired.

It may be observed that, in the case of one of those directions for the priests of Jupiter, form criticism will lead to the modifica-tion of a result reached by other methods. We have seen that a

[1] R.R. 2. 11. 7.   [2] Georgics 1. 259 ff.

number of rules are of the type *oportet, necessum est,* 'it is proper, needful', by which reference is made to a higher authority. From an inquiry into the divine will, that is, some actions emerge as correct, others as incorrect. Again, there are rules in the present indicative, 'A priest does this, does not do that'—a form intended to stimulate the self-respect of the addressee as a member of a select body. What is demanded of him is represented as his natural, noble conduct. Both forms, *oportet* and the indicative, are well suited to this collection. An imperative or jussive, on the other hand, would introduce an entirely different note. It would, in fact, be out of place.

There is, however, one apparent exception: *Capillum Dialis nisi qui liber homo est non detonset.*[1] Landgraf maintains[2] that this is an instance of *non* with the present subjunctive, a jussive, the negation being emphatic. That is to say, he translates: 'Unless a man be free, let him not cut the hair—he must on no account cut the hair—of a priest of Jupiter.'

But there are two things to be said on this. First, even if Landgraf's view were established beyond dispute, the jussive might perhaps be accounted for by the fact that this particular prohibition concerns laymen rather than the priests themselves. It is the unfree among the former who must abstain from a certain action. The prohibition, that is, might be said to be addressed, not to the chosen, but to ordinary people—hence the jussive.

Secondly, Landgraf is very probably wrong. We do not seem to have to do with a jussive at all. The verb *detonso* from which he proceeds occurs nowhere else in Latin literature. So instead of regarding *detonset* as a subjunctive of *detonso*, with the unusual negation *non*, we are quite free to regard it as an indicative of *detonseo*. Or better still, since *detonseo* also is to be met nowhere else, we may emend and read *detondet*; the verb *detondeo* is frequent enough. Either course results in: 'Unless a man be free, he does not cut the hair of a priest of Jupiter.' It is a rule using the indicative, in perfect harmony with the spirit of the

---

[1] 10. 15. 11.
[2] *Historische Grammatik*, vol. iii, pt. 1, 1903, 136.

code.[1] It looks, then, as if the passage ought no longer to be adduced as evidence of *non* with the subjunctive.

[1] Note that 10. 15. 21 also is to some extent addressed to laymen, not belonging to the select company of the priests, and yet the indicative is employed: 'No one takes his place at table above a priest', *Super flaminem haut quisquam alius accumbit.*

4. Judgment: 'he appears to have offended'

To return to law proper, though not yet to legislation—in Republican times, a judge pronouncing on the truth of a charge says: *fecisse, non fecisse, videtur,* 'he appears (not) to have committed the deed'. Why not simply: 'he has (not) committed the deed'?

First, the more elaborate phrase acknowledges the possibility of an error. Normally, the person charged will maintain his innocence, and the judge must choose between two versions. He may choose wrongly. Moreover, though on occasion his concern is with bare facts—as when 'a woman appears to have drunk more wine without her husband's knowledge than was necessary for her health'[1]—quite often it is with points of law as well—as when 'Sthenius appears to have forged an official document'.[2] No doubt Verres, who gave this decision, treated facts and law with equal indifference. But the most decent governor is liable to form a mistaken view not only about what the accused did in fact do, but also as to how far his deed may be described in law as forgery. It is evidently safer to declare: 'he appears to have forged.'

Cicero noticed the admission of fallibility inherent in this verdict. He speaks of 'the caution of our ancestors who required a jury to represent what they had ascertained not as having been done, but as appearing'.[3] For Mommsen, this explanation is sufficient.[4] Cicero, however, had a reason for singling out this aspect: it suited the theory of knowledge he wished to propound. He may well have been aware of other factors which had contributed to the form in question. In any case, such factors existed.

[1] Pliny, Hist. Nat. 14. 14. 90. Exactly what kind of process it was that ended in this condemnation may be left open.

[2] Cicero, Verr. 2. 2. 38. 93.

[3] Acad. 2. 47. 146.

[4] *Römisches Strafrecht,* 1899, 448 f.

Secondly, then, the pronouncement 'he appears' and so on claims to be the result of investigation and evaluation. There is an intimate connexion between this positive claim and the renunciation of flawlessness just discussed. If the use of 'to appear' implies a prudent admission of a possible slip, it at the same time implies that a careful inquiry has taken place. The admission would make no sense but against the background of such an inquiry. 'He appears (not) to have committed the deed' means: 'having weighed the available data, I am led to conclude that he has (not) committed the deed.'

Thirdly, by saying 'he appears' and so on instead of 'he has done' or 'he has not done', a judge keeps aloof from and above the matter. His is a well-considered, sober utterance. An unrestrained 'he has done' might come from the mouth of an accuser or critic, a 'he has not done' from the accused or his defence. In English, scholarly style, 'so-and-so seems to be the case' ('the new system seems to have brought with it no change in the proceedings *apud iudicem*') is sometimes put less in order to express a conscientious doubt than as a sign of detachment.

A fairly close parallel is provided by the language of the augurs. Where straightforward observations are reported, they are reported as facts, without qualification by 'to appear'. (The question 'Tell me if silence appears to prevail', with the answer 'Silence appears to prevail', is no exception. The silence referred to is of a technical nature, and Cicero emphasizes that only a trained person can decide whether it exists. The dialogue goes on: 'Tell me if the chickens eat', 'They eat'—not 'appear to eat'.[1]) On the other hand, in an opinion, especially one concerning the validity of an act, 'to appear' is the proper term to use. True, in the accounts of opinions preserved to us, it is sometimes omitted. Livy tells us that *vitio diem dictam esse augures decreverunt*,[2] though the decree probably ran: 'The day appears to have been faultily set.' Again, by the end of the Republic, as may be seen from Cicero, an augur himself, the form has largely broken down—a corollary of the inner decay of augural institutions. One of his laws is: *Quaeque augur iniusta, nefasta, vitiosa, dira*

---

[1] Div. 2. 34. 74.   [2] 45. 12. 10; the reading is not quite certain.

defixerit, inrita infectaque sunto.[1] But the original role of 'to appear' is unmistakable since, more often than not, the characteristic feature of the form persists in historical works. Surely, when Livy records that the augurs held *vitiosum videri dictatorem*,[2] this reflects the actual wording of the decision. A writer would be inclined to drop rather than insert *videri*.

Another passage is illuminating.[3] In 215 B.C. the plebeian Sempronius was consul, yet the people elected another plebeian his colleague. As he was entering on his office it thundered. The augurs pronounced him *vitio creatum videri*, and the senators gave out that the appointment of two plebeians *deis cordi non esse*. Significantly, the augurs employ 'to appear', the senators do not. The augurs deliver an opinion. That is to say, first, they do not pretend to absolute certainty; secondly, they declare the result of such facts as they have been able to establish and of their subsumption under the appropriate technical category; and thirdly, they disclaim any direct interest—so much so that they speak only of 'a flaw' in general, without touching on the real, political issue. Hence: 'the election of the second consul appears to suffer from a defect'. The senators talk politics. They do pretend to certainty; they do not allude to a search into the facts and their meaning; nor do they profess neutrality—they do specify the defect, the second consul's affiliation. Hence: 'the election of two plebeian consuls is displeasing to the gods'.

It can be shown that the form analysed is not deceptive. There are other circumstances pointing to a fundamental affinity between an opinion of the augurs and a judgment. The augurs, for example, were bound to take evidence in the way in which ordinary courts did it;[4] and in the municipal charter of Osuna they are actually credited with *iurisdictio iudicatio*.[5]

A contrast to both judgment and the expertise of augurs is supplied by the reasons which a censor gives for a *nota*. Of the large number of texts describing the activities of censors, not one says that 'they pronounced a person to appear to have done

---

[1] 2. 8. 21. Cp. Div. 2. 35. 74, Nat. Deor. 2. 4. 10 f.
[2] 8. 23. 14; cp. 8. 15. 6. [3] 23. 31. 13.
[4] Livy 8. 23. 15; Mommsen, *Staatsrecht*, vol. i, 115, n. 3.
[5] *Lex Ursonensis*, ch. 66, in Bruns, 125; Mommsen, 116, n. 3.

so and so'. (Gellius[1] gives an extract from Sabinus, about a certain reply made to the censors which 'appeared, *visum est*, to be lacking in respect'. This expression, however, does not justify the conclusion that the censors declared: 'You appear to have answered disrespectfully.' Its import is that, whatever the writer or reader may think of the reply, those strict censors treated it as intolerable.) The usual phraseology is 'they pronounced a person to have attacked the commonwealth',[2] which presupposes a statement by the censors, 'You have attacked the commonwealth'; or 'they degraded a person because he had an excessive amount of table silver',[3] which presupposes a statement, 'Because you have an excessive amount'—in fact, a direct quotation of a censor's speech, 'Because you have neglected the set sacrifices', has come down to us.[4] Naturally, slight modifications occur, such as 'they degraded a person because they had learned that he had an excessive amount of silver',[5] which presupposes 'Because we have learned that you have an excessive amount'. It may also be observed that it is only when informing the culprit of the reasons that the censor will say 'You have attacked the commonwealth'; the entry in the list must be in the third person, 'He has attacked'. The main point is unaffected: the absence of 'to appear'.

The censor, as supervisor of the nation's moral life, has wide discretionary powers. So first, he is confident that his summing up of the situation is correct; he sees no need for a hesitant 'to appear'. Secondly, he sees no need for referring to a meticulous judicial inquiry. Such an inquiry is not essential. Admittedly, many authors speak of a *censorium iudicium* or the like[6]— even Cicero,[7] who, where he defends a client for whom it is important that a *nota* should be of little account, criticizes this

---

[1] 4. 20. 11.   [2] Livy 24. 18. 4.

[3] Livy, epit. 14, Gellius 4. 8. 7. Cp. Livy 4. 24. 7, 29. 37. 9, 10, 14, Valerius Maximus 2. 9. 2, 5, 7, Velleius Paterculus 2. 10. 1, Asconius, Tog. cand. 84 (Orelli), Suetonius, Aug. 39, Gellius 4. 20. 6. In Greek *quod* becomes ὅτι: Plutarch, Cato Maior 17. 7.   [4] Festus 344.

[5] Gellius 17. 21. 39. In 4. 8. 7 and Livy, epit. 14, the commoner form is followed, 'because he had too much table silver'. The presumption is that the less common expression reflects the earliest report.

[6] E.g. Varro, L.L. 6. 71.   [7] E.g. Rep. 4. 6.

usage as misleading and late.[1] But the criticism, though interested, is sound. It is noteworthy that *censorium iudicium*, however frequent, is not to be met with in any law, senatusconsult
or edict; and a statute which introduced a proper trial in
58 B.C. but was abolished in 52[2] proves only that no proper trial
was requisite either before or after. Thirdly, 'to appear' would
be out of place in the censor's statement since, far from adopting
a detached attitude, he is personally involved. It is his right
and duty to enforce his standards of civic conduct. 'You have
attacked the commonwealth' is not intended as a cool pronouncement on the truth or otherwise of a charge defined by
law, but as a severe reprimand for slighting those principles
which the censor feels called on to uphold. I argued above that,
in contradistinction to the reticent 'He appears to have done
so and so', which betokens impartiality, the violent 'He has done
so and so' smacks of accusation or rebuke. A remark by Livy
confirms that a censor's style in telling a person why he has
branded him is basically the same as the style used by an
accuser who demands that a person should be branded. Cato,
Livy says,[3] made a speech against a senator whom he had
branded so passionate that, 'even had he delivered it as accuser
before the *nota* instead of as censor after the *nota*', nothing could
have saved the man from losing his seat.

It is an interesting paradox that a judgment, with its caution
and moderation, enjoys a higher degree of recognition than the
censor's unqualified verdict. The finding 'He appears to have
done so and so' is objective, the person of the judge has nothing
to do with it. Within its self-imposed limits, it is essentially of
permanent validity. By contrast, the statement 'You have done
so and so' expresses the censor's personal view. It contains no
reservations, it claims more than is necessarily warranted. But
it is essentially valid only for the period of the *lustrum*.

[1] Pro Clu. 42 ff.; Mommsen, *Staatsrecht*, vol. ii, pt. 1, 385 ff.
[2] Dio Cassius 38. 13, 40. 57.
[3] 39. 42. 7.

5. Motivation, Ruling and Aim in Senatusconsults

I⊤ may be worth while to inspect a form of legislation rather more sophisticated than any we have considered so far; more sophisticated and, significantly, more ephemeral. I am referring to a curious tripartite structure shown by two senatusconsults about the middle of the first century A.D.[1]

As Mommsen pointed out,[2] the earliest extant senatusconsults to divide the resolution into motivation, introduced by *cum*, and main operative part, introduced by *placere*, are those of 11 B.C., dealing with aqueducts.[3] He might have mentioned a senatusconsult *de ludis saecularibus*[4] of 17 B.C. as getting very near the new form: *Censuerunt ut, quoniam res ita se habet, liceat*, 'They have voted that, since such and such is the case, a certain action should be allowed.' It only remained to insert *placere* before the actual decision, *liceat*, and transpose *ut* after *placere*, to arrive at the full division. At any rate, from that time onwards, the division remained the normal thing. Previously, the motivation had not been marked off. It was implied either in the main operative part itself, or in a summary, commonly prefixed to senatusconsults, of the speech by which the question had been opened in the senate, *quod verba facta sunt* and so on.

I do not propose to investigate in detail the background of the division. It may suffice to draw attention to three points. First, as a senatusconsult is addressed not to the people at large but to a magistrate (at least in the early Principate that is still the position), its language is much freer and more general than that of statutes or edicts. It is not intended as a precise guide for the ordinary man, but as advice for an official, who will be quite capable of judging exactly how far and in what

---

[1] Cp. Daube, *Savigny-Stiftung* 65, 1947, *Rom. Abt.*, 287 ff.
[2] *Staatsrecht*, vol. iii, pt. 2, 1888, 1008 f.
[3] A specimen in Bruns, 193.   [4] Bruns, 191 f.

way to follow it out. A great deal, that is, must be left to the discretion of the recipient. For this reason, it is essential that he should be acquainted with the motives behind it—otherwise he might go very wrong. A statute or edict, giving scrupulously detailed orders or information, may dispense with motives. In a senatusconsult, they must from the outset have been of the greatest importance, even though for a considerable period they were, as we have seen, mixed up with the main part or the summary of the speech that had opened the debate.

Secondly, that at a certain stage the motivation was assigned a place of its own is hardly surprising. It was a natural step making for greater clarity. The magistrate had no longer to deduce the senate's ideas from the actual provision or the speech prefixed to the resolution. The resolution now contained two separate parts, the first setting out the motives, the second the main desire of the senate. I have already remarked[1] that even now the motivation constituted an integral element of the senatusconsult, on a level with the principal rule. There are cases where it can be demonstrated that the motivation was looked upon as prohibiting an act and the principal rule as sanctioning this prohibition.

Thirdly, though the division into motivation and actual provision was a natural step to take, very possibly certain speculations of the rhetoricians helped to bring it about. It may be recalled that Cicero, in his De Legibus,[2] adopts Plato's idea that a lawgiver should preface his laws by an outline of their function, in order that they may be obeyed from conviction rather than from fear. More precisely, he adopts one half of it, namely, the general introduction to an entire section of a code. For example, the chapter in which he lists his religious statutes is preceded by a eulogy of the gods. In Plato, in addition to the requirement of a general 'prelude' to a section, we find that of a motivation for each single statute.[3] Thus a law concerning wounding runs:[4] 'If a man, intending to kill another, only wounds him, he deserves no pity, but is to be regarded as a

---

[1] See above, pp. 29 f.
[3] Laws 4. 723 B.
[2] 2. 6. 14 ff., 3. 1. 1 ff.
[4] 9. 876 E f.

murderer; only out of respect for his escape from ill-fortune, he shall be relieved of the death-penalty and be deported for life.' Cicero does not take over this part of Plato's scheme. After the general 'prelude' to a section, he states the laws of that section without any specific explanations. To be sure, he then goes through the statutes enumerated one by one, setting forth their history and purpose. But this commentary is no longer thought of as part of the legislation, it is thought of as belonging to the lawgiver's conversation with his friends. However, it is not unlikely that Cicero's remarks led to an increased interest in the question of motivation. The De Legibus was published after 44 B.C. The first known senatusconsult dividing the resolution into motivation and actual rule dates from about thirty years later. There may well have been some influence of rhetorical discussion on the draftsmen of the senate.

But it is a further development which deserves notice. In two senatusconsults, the *Trebellianum* and the *Macedonianum*,[1] the resolution is divided not into two parts, motivation and chief decision, but into three, motivation, introduced by *cum*, chief decision, introduced by *placere*, and ultimate aim, introduced by *quo magis* or *ut*.

The *Trebellianum*, in its motivation, says that once an heir has transferred the inheritance to a fideicommissary, equity demands that the latter, not the former, should be sued by creditors of the estate. It goes on to enjoin (if, for the moment, we accept the present version) that actions normally available against and in favour of the heir should in this case be given against and in favour of the fideicommissary. Then the wider purpose of the decree is stated: 'In order that, in future, the last wishes of the deceased may be ratified.'

This clause refers to the fact that, before the senatusconsult, if a *fideicommissum* embraced the whole or the greater part of an inheritance, the heir would prefer to abstain rather than run the risk of having to pay the testator's debts and possibly getting no reimbursement from the fideicommissary. The consequence of an abstention was that the *fideicommissum* also was destroyed.

[1] Bruns, 202 f.

The senate expresses the hope that, as a result of its action, heirs will no longer hesitate to enter under wills with *fideicommissa.* That things did not, in fact, quite work out this way is another matter: heirs wanted not only to incur no risk but also to obtain some positive benefit. The point is that a separate part is assigned to the ultimate, indirect effect the decree is expected to produce.

The very fact that exactly the same tripartite form recurs in the *Macedonianum* proves that we have to do with a carefully chosen, artistic device. The *Macedonianum* gives as reason for its rule the pernicious influence of loans on criminal characters like Macedo. There follows the rule that a loan to a *filiusfamilias* should not be actionable even after the death of his *paterfamilias.* The ultimate object is: 'That the usurers who lead people astray[1] may know that no son's debt can become good by waiting for his father's death.'

In the past, a moneylender dealing with a *filiusfamilias* had had an urgent interest in the death of the *paterfamilias*. It would render his claim enforceable, while, if the *filiusfamilias* should die before his *paterfamilias*, he would lose all. Macedo had murdered his father, if not at the instigation of his creditors, at least under great pressure on their part. Henceforth, the senate hopes, in consequence of its regulation, there will be no more temptation for a usurer to work for the death of a *paterfamilias*.

Was there any point in adding a special third part setting forth the wider, indirect effect desired? Theoretically, there is a great deal to be said for it. To put first the immediate reason for the legislation, above all, the weakness of the present state of law, next the new law and finally the ultimate object is a fine, logical arrangement.

Nor can it be denied that, in the two cases under discussion, the part mentioning the wider purpose exercised a considerable influence on the way the new law was applied and elaborated in practice. The magistrates, and the jurists writing for them, extended or restricted the rules in question according as either course would serve the fundamental aims proclaimed.

The *Trebellianum*, for instance, originally referred only to

---

[1] Cp. *malo exemplo vendere* in the *senatusconsultum Hosidianum* (Bruns, 200).

actions already instituted against the testator—i.e. already beyond *litiscontestatio*—at the moment of his death, but not to future actions. Kniep suggested[1] that *ex his eos subire*, which Mommsen regards as a corruption of *eas lites eos subire*, has been substituted for *lites contestatas eos subire*. Maybe *executionem eos subire* is more likely. An abbreviated *executionem* is nearer *ex his*, and Gaius, in discussing the development leading up to the *Trebellianum*, speaks of *hereditarias actiones exequi*.[2] At any rate, future actions did not create such an urgent problem. It was usual for a fideicommissary, when receiving the inheritance, to promise the heir to take his place as defendant in any actions that might be brought, and provided he was honest and solvent, this arrangement would be satisfactory. But no such arrangement was possible in the case of actions already instituted against the testator. Under the ordinary rules, before the *Trebellianum*, these were inevitably continued against the heir—by means of *translatio iudicii* or something like it—who had to rely on being indemnified later by the fideicommissary.[3]

---

[1] *Gai Institutionum Commentarius Secundus 97–289*, 1913, 397 ff.

[2] 2. 252 at the end.

[3] It does not seem to have been observed that even this state of the law, represented by the stipulations *emptae et venditae hereditatis* of G. 2. 252, is the result of an interesting evolution. The clue lies in the recognition that, in the promise to the heir, the part *et omnino si quis cum eo ageret, ut defenderetur* is later than *ut quidquid condemnatus fuisset, eo nomine indemnis esset*; and in the promise to the buyer of an inheritance, *ut etiam pateretur eum exequi* is later than *ut si quid ad heredem pervenisset, id restitueretur*. We must, therefore, distinguish two stages (omitting minor developments) : (1) At first, an heir who sold the inheritance was promised indemnification should he be condemned in an action. The buyer was promised that he would be paid over what the heir obtained in an action (*quanta pecunia*, D. 45. 1. 50. 1, 50. 16. 178 pr.—the Gaian *quid* reflects a liberal widening). These promises included future actions as well as pending ones. (2) Subsequently, there was added the arrangement that the buyer would take the heir's place as defendant or plaintiff. This new arrangement could refer only to future actions. Pending ones, into which it was not possible for the buyer to enter, still came under the older promises of indemnification or paying over. In fact, since future actions were now provided for by the new arrangement, the older promises henceforth had regard exclusively to pending ones. At this second stage, then, the stipulations meant (*a*) a promise to the heir of indemnification should he be condemned in an action coming down from the testator; (*b*) a promise to the buyer that the heir would pay over anything he obtained by such an action; (*c*) a promise to the heir that the buyer would take his place as defendant in future actions; and (*d*) a promise to the buyer that he might take the heir's place as plaintiff in future actions. These stipulations having become usual between heir and fideicommissary, the *Trebellianum* singled out for reform the case most inconvenient for the heir, namely, (*a*).

The senate dealt with the more urgent problem only. It laid down that, on transfer of the inheritance, any pending actions should be continued against the fideicommissary instead of, as before, against the heir. The result was that the heir now had better protection against actions already instituted than against future ones. Of actions already instituted he was relieved by law, whereas, with regard to future actions, his safety still depended on the fideicommissary's honesty and solvency. Presumably it was not long before it was realized that, if heirs were to be induced to co-operate, they must be assured also of full, automatic protection against future actions. So the senatusconsult was interpreted as relieving them of these as well, and indeed, the text itself was altered accordingly—no doubt largely by the classics themselves. Fortunately for us, as usual, they were not very thorough; they left e.g. *si qua iudicia penderent,* 'if any lawsuits are pending'.

There can be little doubt that this extension of the decree was undertaken in pursuance of the third part, the *quo magis*-clause. It became clear to magistrates and jurists that the ultimate object, the 'ratification of the last wishes of the deceased', could be attained—or approached, for there turned out to be other obstacles—only by progressing in this direction.

Far less relevant is a further extension—not so far recognized as such—to the effect that actions available to the heir should also automatically pass to the fideicommissary. The original decree had been only about actions against the heir (or rather, the testator). This further extension was no longer in the heir's interest; it cannot, therefore, be considered as specifically made in view of the *quo magis*-part. It was simply a logical working out and straightening out of the whole position. That, in the text of the senatusconsult as handed down to us, the actions available to the heir are a secondary—though probably classical—insertion is clear, first, from their utter incongruity with the motivation, which speaks only of the necessity of relieving the heir from actions burdening him; secondly, from the change in pronoun, *neque in eos* but *neque his,* and again, *sed his* but *et in eos;* and thirdly, from the change in order, *in heredem heredibusque* and *neque in eos neque his* but *sed his et in eos.* In the account given by Gaius[1] (which does not, however, purport to repeat the decree verbatim) the pronoun is always *is,* and the order always corresponds to *sed his et in eos.* But even here, the missing *ei,* 'to him', which is supplied by all editors—and, indeed, as early as Justinian's Institutes[2]—as having dropped out, may well be an indication that Gaius's precursor had the genuine text before him, where only actions against the heir were mentioned, and that, when he added actions available to him, in one case he forgot to do so.

The *Macedonianum* furnishes an example of a restrictive interpretation proceeding from the third part. The main provision said that a person lending money to a *filiusfamilias* should have no action even after the death of the *paterfamilias.* On general principle, it would have followed that, if a son after his father's death repaid the money by mistake, he could claim it back by *condictio.* The lawyers, however, decided that he could not. The senatusconsult, they held, was not intended to help him in that case.

This limitation has its root in the *ut*-clause, where the ultimate object of the senate is declared to be the elimination of the interest moneylenders formerly had in the death of the *paterfamilias,* or to put it differently, of their interest in getting a son to do away with his father. Obviously, to attain this object, it was quite enough to make it clear to moneylenders that the death of a *paterfamilias* would give them no action. But it was not necessary to grant the son a *condictio* if, after his father had died, he made repayment by mistake: the danger of parricide, or instigation to parricide, no longer existed. Accordingly, contrary to general principle, the *condictio* was not allowed. Note that Marcian distinctly bases this restriction on the third part of the senatusconsult, 'that the usurers may know that the debt will not become good by waiting for the death of the *paterfamilias*', when he explains that *condictio* is refused because the son's defence against an action was introduced, not out of

consideration for him, but 'to thwart his creditor', *in odium
eius cui debetur.*[1]

If, then, the tripartite form is strictly logical, and if the
interpreters of the *Trebellianum* and *Macedonianum* found it ser-
viceable in practice, it may seem strange that it was so short-
lived. The main cause appears to be that it is somewhat too
subtle. The motives and the aims of a legislator, the reasons why
he introduces a reform and the object he has in mind, are so
intimately bound up with one another that it is unnatural to
tear them apart. Modern statutes, if they give a motivation,
normally put in it both the weakness of the present law and the
improvement hoped for: 'Whereas hitherto such and such has
been the case, and whereas it is desirable that in future such and
such should be the case.'

Another consideration is that the separation of motives and
aims by placing the former at the head and the latter last is
hardly feasible where the actual provision in the middle is of
any length. In the *Trebellianum* and *Macedonianum*, the principal,
operative part between motives and aims is very short. If it
were five times as long, a magistrate might well have been per-
plexed. 'Since such and such is the case, it has been decided
that—and then a string of complicated rules—in order that a
certain result may come about': this would be far from lucid.

The *Trebellianum* is of A.D. 56. According to the prevalent
view, the *Macedonianum* was passed between 69 and 79. I have
recently argued in favour of 51;[2] and the fact that the two senatusconsults show the same form, and a form found nowhere else,
may be added to the points supporting this date, which involves
a shorter interval. In all probability, the form is due to one
particular draftsman. It is the creation of an individual, with
no valid setting in communal life, and it failed to take root.
Maybe its author was a student of rhetoric, impressed by speculations concerning the *conclusio*, the summing up, of an exposition. The *Macedonianum* at any rate (which, if of 51, is the older

---

[1] D. 12. 6. 40 pr. Cp. Pomponius in D. 12. 6. 19 pr.: the defence was introduced
'to penalise the creditor', *poenae causa.*

[2] *Savigny-Stiftung* 65, 1947, *Rom. Abt.*, 308 ff. See above, p. 30.

of the two) contains other features manifestly deriving from rhetorical doctrine—such as the notion of causes for a crime springing from a man's nature, and the distinction between these causes and those springing from his position in life, his fortune, in this case, his debts.

6. Survival of Forms in New Settings

HERE are a few illustrations of that curious—and, for us, fortunate—phenomenon I have mentioned several times: the tenaciousness of forms, their power of survival even when transplanted to alien soil.

In the Republic and early Principate, the Roman senate cannot pass laws. Its function is to give advice to magistrates; and however authoritative such advice may be, it is not, in strictness, legislation. Accordingly, as regards form, the senate does not command. It uses, not the future imperative typical of statutes, 'this or that shall be done', but expressions like 'the senate holds that this or that should be done', *censere* or *placere* with an accusative and infinitive or a subjunctive.

As is well known, the form occurs even in the later Principate, when the senate does possess legislative power. In a sense, this is in itself a striking example of a form persisting though it has long ceased to correspond to reality. And when we assess the merits or otherwise of form criticism, we may do well to reflect that, even if all direct information respecting the earlier position of the senate were lost to us, we could still deduce a good deal from the form of some of the later decrees.

However, this dragging on of a form after its time is passed is not the kind of thing I have in mind at present. What I wish to demonstrate is that, where material is transferred from one domain to another, say, from statutes to senatusconsults or from expert advice to edicts, the original form is apt to survive. It follows, as a corollary of this proposition, that if a form is out of keeping with its present surroundings, this is frequently a sign of the material having originated in a different milieu.

A. Imperatives in Senatusconsults

Let us begin with a case already noted by Ihering,[1] who has contributed more than anyone to a proper appreciation of the

[1] *Geist*, vol. ii, pt. 2, 6th and 7th ed., 1923, 608, n. 828.

significance of legal forms. In the *senatusconsultum Orphitianum*,[1] a future imperative does appear instead of a more cautious form. This senatusconsult gives children the first claim in succession to their mother, adding that if none of them accepts, 'the old state of law shall prevail', *ius antiquum esto*. The imperative cannot be accounted for by saying that, by A.D. 178, the senate passed real laws and therefore deliberately chose the form of statutes. For another clause of the same senatusconsult which is preserved puts the traditional, advisory subjunctive: cases already settled at the time of the decree, the senate holds, 'should remain unaffected', *rata maneant*.

The explanation must be that the imperative was taken over together with some material from certain statutes, and it is clear that these were the *lex Julia* and *lex Papia Poppaea*. They had introduced important innovations in the law of succession, but in connexion with several of them they had defined circumstances in which there should be no change but the old law, the old rights, should remain. Here the clause *ius antiquum esto* was perfectly appropriate, and there is adequate evidence that it did occur. The phrase *ius antiquum* is constantly employed by the jurists in discussing this reform,[2] and from their quotations of other portions of the two statutes[3] it may be seen that, as one would expect, any rules were couched in the future imperative.

The senatusconsult under notice, then, in laying down a provision on the model of those statutes, left intact the original form even though it did not fit the new context at all. The form survived the transfer from statutes to senatusconsult, and now betrays immediately the dependence of the latter on the former.

There is only one other senatusconsult, *de Aphrodisiensibus*,[4] with the imperative, and the circumstances are very similar. We possess only a Greek version, contained in a letter by Mark Antony to the people of Aphrodisias; but, as usual, the original Latin is faithfully reflected.

The senatusconsult says that it has been resolved—ἀρέσκειν,

[1] Bruns, 211.
[2] Ulp. 1. 21, 17. 2, 18. 1, C. 6. 51. 1. 1 b.
[3] Bruns, 115 f.
[4] Bruns, 185 ff.

corresponding to *placere*—that the Aphrodisians should be free—
ἐλευθέρους εἶναι, *liberos esse*. It has further been resolved—
ἀρέσκειν—that their freedom should be of the highest kind
possible for allies. Now follows an abrupt switching over to the
imperative: 'Their temple of Venus shall be a sanctuary under
the same rules as the temple of Diana at Ephesus, and any
temple in the precincts shall also be a sanctuary', τόπος ἄσυλος
ἔστω, *locus asylos esto*. In the next paragraph the decree returns to
ὅπως, *ut*, with the subjunctive, quite common after ἀρέσκειν,
placere, in senatusconsults: 'that they should continue in enjoy-
ment of their dependencies', ὅπως ἔχωσιν.

The imperative in the section concerning the right of asylum,
besides causing a break in the syntax, is contrary to the spirit
of a senatusconsult. What happened is that the senate, in
ratifying this privilege, mechanically adopted the form that was
customary in the constitution of a temple, in a *lex templo dicta*,
namely, the form of statutes, of *leges*, the future imperative. That
the right of asylum in particular, where it was laid down, was
laid down in this form is confirmed by Servius, the commen-
tator on Virgil. He tells us[1] that the right is restricted to temples
quibus consecrationis lege concessum est, 'to which it has been granted
by the statute of dedication'. One of many parallels to the mention of the rules of another temple—here that of Diana at
Ephesus—is this clause, from the constitution of an altar at
Salona[2]: 'The remaining statutes concerning this altar shall
be the same as those concerning that of Diana on the Aventine',
*ceterae leges eaedem sunto quae arae Dianae sunt in Aventino monte
dictae*. Note again the future imperative.

The case is particularly instructive, seeing that the form in

---

[1] *Aen.* 2. 761.
[2] See Wissowa, *Religion der Römer*, 2nd ed., 1912, 473, n. 6. He asserts (op. cit. 39)
that whenever the constitution of one temple refers in this way to that of another,
it is to that of the temple of Diana on the Aventine. The senatusconsult under discussion, however, shows that, in the Greek area, the temple of Diana at Ephesus
might be quoted as model. As regards the privilege of a sanctuary, even if no other
considerations had spoken in favour of naming Ephesus, the temple on the
Aventine could not possibly have been named, since it had not that privilege. But
Ephesus was famous for it: see Tacitus, *Ann.* 3. 61—'The Ephesians were the first
of all to appear' (before the senators who investigated the claims of temples).

question has here resisted not only the passage of the idea from a temple statute to a senatusconsult, but also the translation of the latter from Latin into Greek.

Before going on to the next example, I ought perhaps to say that the *lex de imperio Vespasiani*[1] does not belong here. To be sure, by far the greater part of what is preserved shows the style of senatusconsults—*ut liceat*, 'Vespasian should be allowed the same privileges as his predecessors' and so forth—while the future imperative is confined to the last clause entitled *sanctio*— 'if anyone transgresses another statute because of this one, he shall not be accountable', *ne fraudi esto*. At first sight one might be tempted to suppose that the makers of the statute were so deeply influenced by ideas expressed in senatusconsults that, together with the ideas, they adopted the form—just as the makers of the *senatusconsultum Orphitianum* or the *senatusconsultum de Aphrodisiensibus*, in provisions inspired by the *leges Julia* and *Papia Poppaea*, or by a *lex templo dicta*, adopted the form of statutes.

In actual fact, however, what we find in the *lex de imperio Vespasiani* is straightforward quotation, not use of a form in an inappropriate setting. More precisely, the statute quotes the senate's resolution concerning the position of the new emperor, in order to add to it legislative, popular ratification. No doubt Mommsen is right in assuming[2] that the opening clause, which is lost, must, like the *sanctio*, have been in the imperative: 'Vespasian shall (not: should) have tribunician power, *tribunicia potestate esto*, in the manner set forth by the senate as follows.' Quite naturally, the section beginning at this point repeats the words of the senatusconsult in question. Then, in the *sanctio*, which was apparently not postulated by the senate, and is marked off by a special heading, the statute once more returns to the future imperative.

There is here nothing remarkable from the point of view of form. The *lex* as such employs the future imperative; and the subjunctive, *ut liceat*, occurs in a part clearly ascribed to its author, the senate. This part, the quotation, is longer than the

[1] Bruns, 202 f. See Mommsen, *Staatsrecht*, vol. ii, pt. 2, 3rd ed., 1887, 876 ff.
[2] 878, n. 2.

rest. But why not? It was not pretended that the *lex* was anything but acceptance of the plan worked out by the senate.
The case cannot be compared to the *senatusconsultum Orphitianum* or *de Aphrodisiensibus*, which states one of its own rules by
means of the future imperative, out of place in a senatusconsult.

B. *Imperatives in the Edict of the Aediles*

But there are quite a few cases which can be compared;
among them another one of the future imperative appearing
where it obviously ought not to—and again the explanation
lies in the permanence of forms. Indeed, for once, form criticism will disclose not only the original milieu of the rules in
question, but even—though with less certainty—the actual
person at whose initiative they were taken over from one domain
into the other. I am referring to the Edict of the curule aediles,[1]
which ordains that those who offer slaves or cattle for sale
'shall proclaim publicly and accurately' any serious defects,
palam recte pronuntianto, dicunto.[2]

The aediles—and the praetor—can legislate in the strict
sense no more than the senate. They are entitled to issue directions which, during their year of office, must be followed. But
this is not legislation, not even in the case of the praetor, who
has *imperium* whereas the aediles have not. Consequently, among
the very large number of praetorian and aedilician directions
which have come down to us, there are none in the future
imperative, the form distinguishing statutes proper—except
where the sale of slaves and cattle is concerned. In all others,
the form used is *ut* or *ne* with the subjunctive. Actually, even of
the rules concerning the sale of slaves and cattle, some show the
subjunctive; which renders the imperatives all the more curious.

It is an old puzzle. It has been said[3] that the imperatives
reflect the nature of these provisions as police-measures, concerned with public order. But this theory will not do. From the

---

[1] Lenel, 555, 565.

[2] Cp. also *ea omnia in venditione pronuntianto*, 'all this they shall proclaim when
selling them', and *de cetero quoque pecore faciunto*, 'they shall do so also in the case of
other cattle'—scil. than beasts of draught.

[3] E.g. by Karlowa, *Römische Rechtsgeschichte*, vol. i, 1885, 462.

general philological point of view, there is nothing whatever in the future imperative making it particularly suitable for police rules. And as for legal usage, on the one hand, statutes proper employ the form no matter whether they smack of the police or not. *Si agnatus nec escit, gentiles familiam habento,*[1] 'If there is no agnate, the *gentiles* shall take the inheritance', is no police-measure, yet it has the future imperative. On the other hand, there are plenty of edictal rules in the nature of police-measures besides those about slaves and cattle, yet we never meet with the future imperative. *Ne quis eum qui in ius vocabitur vi eximat,*[2] 'No one may forcibly deliver a person summoned to court', is very much concerned with public order; so is the aedilician edict, which we have already considered,[3] about beasts kept on a road that is in common use. But the form is *ne* with the subjunctive.

It is noteworthy that a very early version of the edict respecting slaves is recorded by Gellius,[4] and here, too, the imperative appears: 'See to it that the label of each slave is so written that any defect may be accurately known', *titulus scriptus sit curato ita ut intellegi recte possit quid morbi vitiive cuique sit*. There are here, indeed, several further surprising features. Not only is the rule expressed by means of an imperative; the imperative is in the singular, and, what is more, it seems to be in the second person: *curato*, 'see to it'. Admittedly it is possible to treat it as in the third, 'he shall see to it' (in the original context, the subject, the vendor of a slave, may have been named in the preceding sentence), or even as impersonal, 'one shall see to it' (that in ancient Latin the so-called third person singular may be impersonal is too often forgotten, with queer propositions resulting[5]). Even so, the form would be odd enough. The second person, however, is more likely. But what could have induced the curule aediles to deviate so far from the usual diction of their Edict? What could have induced them to put *curato*, 'see to it', instead of *ut curent*, 'they should see to it'?

[1] Bruns, 23.   [2] Lenel, 73 f.
[3] See above, p. 27.   [4] 4. 2. 1.
[5] Cp. above, pp. 57 ff.

Again, why this pedantic circumlocution—certainly not the kind of thing typical of the police—'see to it that the label is so written', instead of a straight 'write the label so' or 'the label must be so written'? This sentence, 'the label of each slave see to it (or: one shall see to it) that it is so written' etc., sounds much more like technical advice as to the correct, decent mode of conducting a sale than like a request of a magistrate.

Nor is this impression misleading. All questions we have put can be answered if we remember that there is also a non-legal branch of ancient Roman literature where the imperative of statutes, the future imperative ending in *to*, is frequent—namely, the writings on husbandry.

Cato's Agriculture contains some 200 such imperatives: 'Begin to trim the olive-yard before the vernal equinox', *incipito putare*.[1] Naturally, these works discuss various contracts and the considerations of convenience and decency to be taken into account in concluding them. Cato's very first instruction is:[2] 'When you think of acquiring a farm, keep this in mind— *sic in animo habeto*—that you should spare no pains in examining it'. In another passage, he tells you how to measure out wine to a buyer:[3] 'Make a hole in the bottom of the cask, fit a pipe' etc., *pertundito, subdito*. Again, he who undertakes the gathering of olives for the owner 'shall give security for the proper harvesting', *satisdato*,[4] while the purchaser of olives on the tree 'shall make a promise and give security to ensure proper payment', *recte haec dari promittito satisque dato*.[5] Here we are getting fairly near the sort of provision to be found in the Edict of the aediles. The following example is even closer.[6] The section concerning the sale of a winter pasturage opens: *Qua vendas fini dicito*, 'State the boundaries of the pasturage you are selling'. The aediles require that the defects of the object should be stated.

The conclusion is plain. The imperatives in the aedilician Edict derive from the treatises on husbandry. Their original setting in life is not in the court of the aediles nor, indeed, in any statutes—how could it have been there?—but in a circle

[1] 44. [2] 1. 1. [3] 154.
[4] 144. 2. [5] 146. 2. [6] 149. 1.

of technical experts, whose suggestions deserved to be made part of the law. The teachers of husbandry, that is, recommended certain ways of negotiating an agreement, and the aediles announced that they would give actions if these were disregarded.

Whether they took the rules direct from some work now lost, or whether they—or the men they consulted—merely composed them under the influence of the literature in question, we need not decide. Nor need we decide whether all the imperatives occurring in Julian's redaction go back to the oldest version of this section or whether, as is more probable, only one or two of them do and the others were added later, be it in analogy to the earlier ones or again from writings on management. What matters is, first, as far as history is concerned, the origin of the aedilician directions about the sale of slaves and cattle in that specific milieu of learned writers; and secondly, as far as our methods of research are concerned, the fact that this origin is revealed by a form which has remained unaffected by the transition from one sphere to another. The diction of the manual is taken over into the order given by the magistrate.

A third detail deserves notice. Though the future imperative was common enough in daily life, in all probability the writers who introduced it into technical works were consciously imitating the language of statutes. Remember that Cato also uses the form 'No one should wish to have done so and so'.[1] They assumed something of the role of a lawgiver. They meant to indicate that the well-tried, traditional way of doing things—of planting, of grafting, of building—which they described was to be respected almost as if it were sanctioned by law. So the development leading up to the aedilician Edict took place in three stages. At first the statutes used this imperative. Afterwards the authors of manuals deliberately borrowed it. And then, when the aediles drew on the manuals, they failed to adapt the form to the new context.

It is, then, the connexion of the Edict of the aediles with the treatises on management which accounts for the imperatives.

[1] See above, p. 47.

It also accounts for some of them being in the plural and others in the singular. The same happens in those treatises— e.g. he who undertakes the gathering of olives for the owner 'shall gather properly', *cogito recte*, and all those he employs 'shall swear that they have not stolen any fruit', *iuranto*.[1] It also accounts for some of them being in the third person and others in the second, and for the imperative form appearing side by side with subjunctives. We may compare: 'Lay down a meadow, supplied with water if you have it; a suburban farm he (or: one) should furnish with the utmost skill', *pratum si inrigivum habebis summittito, fundum suburbanum ita paret uti quam soller-tissimum habeat*.[2] Of course, it is possible that, in the original version of the edict, all imperatives were in the same number and person, and that there were no subjunctives with them. But on the basis of the view here advanced, it is not necessary to postulate such uniformity.

Above all, the didactic *titulus scriptus sit curato ita*, 'the label of each slave see to it that it is written in the proper manner', no longer creates any difficulty. This is exactly what must be expected in a guide. 'See to it', says Cato,[3] 'that the oxen drink good water', *boves aquam bonam bibant curato*. One of his rules for the overseer is:[4] 'The housekeeper see to it that she performs all her duties', *vilicae quae sunt officia curato faciat*. Note that in both passages *curato* is construed with the simple subjunctive—i.e. without *ut*—just as in the edict under discussion, and that the arrangement of the words also is similar.

So far, I think, we are on safe ground. I will now hazard the conjecture that it was Cato himself who, when aedile in 199, prompted the publication of the earliest edict on the sale of slaves. I say 'he prompted its publication', not 'he published it', for he was not a curule aedile but only a plebeian one and, as such, lacked the right to issue edicts. (For this reason alone, the edict could not possibly have been named after him. But even a curule aedile was never connected with an edict in the

---

[1] 144. 2.　　　　　　　　[2] 8. 1 f.　　　　　　　　[3] 73.

[4] 143. 1. Cp. also 2. 5, 'Any remaining tasks it is best to see to it that they are performed', *curare* (infinitive for imperative) *uti perficiantur*, and 67. 1, 'Those about the press should see to it that the olives are well dried', *curent uti olea bene siccetur*.

same personal way as a praetor, since while the latter published his edict single-handed, the two curule aediles published theirs jointly.) That the style of the edict is indistinguishable from Cato's I have already pointed out. Clearly, its spirit, too, is that of the fighter for strict honesty, the future censor; the very year after, in 198, as governor of Sardinia, he drove out the usurers and, unlike his predecessors, refused to charge either the Roman treasury or the province with the cost of any luxuries.[1] Moreover, as has long been seen, he is the first to be quoted as commenting on the edict;[2] and the edict cannot be much older.

Perhaps the following consideration is the most suggestive. If Cato was not the first to borrow the imperative of the statutes for regular use in technical manuals—I have a strong feeling that he was—at least he employed the form more enthusiastically than anyone else. After him, it fades out. In Varro it does not occur at all, in Columella and Pliny very rarely. If we proceed from this basis, there seems no choice but to regard Cato's works as the source behind the edict; and as we know that it goes back to his period, it is not an unlikely assumption that he had a hand in it when he held the office of aedile himself.

Supposing this result—that Cato in 199 brought about the promulgation of this edict—is correct, it has a bearing on various other dates.

To begin with, we must then hold that he had by that time, when he was thirty-five years of age, fully worked out the peculiar legal style of his technical rules which characterizes his De Agricultura; it is precisely the presence of this style in the edict which betrays his ultimate authorship. Now the general view, which goes back to Mommsen,[3] is that he did not start writing till he was a very old man. However, both the passages on which this view rests significantly omit any mention of the practical manuals.

Cornelius Nepos records[4] that 'though he took up the study of letters as an old man, yet he made such progress that it

---

[1] Livy 32. 27. 3 f., Plutarch, Cato Maior 6. 2.
[2] D. 21. 1. 10. 1. See e.g. Jolowicz, *Historical Introduction*, 2nd ed., 1952, 307 n. 7.
[3] *Römische Geschichte*, 10th ed., 1907, vol. i, 926.   [4] Cato 3. 2.

would not be easy to find anything concerning Greek or Italian affairs that was unknown to him'. The reference here is to the systematic occupation with literature, antiquities and the like. Nothing is said that would exclude the writing of guides or, say, speeches long before this. In fact, in the following sentence Nepos continues, without any sense of contradiction—and, indeed, there is none: 'From his youth he composed speeches; when an old man, he began to write his Histories (the Origins).'[1]

The other text adduced by Mommsen is from Cicero.[2] He represents the aged Cato as engaged on the seventh book of his Origins, as collecting historical records, as revising the speeches he had delivered in famous cases, as going into secular and sacred law and as studying Greek literature. This tallies well with Nepos's account. Not a word of technical treatises.

We are free, therefore, to assume that the De Agricultura— or some other handbook of this type—is an early production, presumably based on his experience on his father's farm. The wider interests came later.

The dating of the Merchant by Plautus is also affected. Hitherto there has seemed to be no indication of its date. But it contains what is almost certainly an allusion to the edict under notice.[3] So now we have at least a *terminus ante quem non*. It cannot have been produced before 199.

C. 'It appears to be proper' and 'it is my opinion' in the Edict of the Praetor

The aediles went for advice to the experts on husbandry, a fact coming out in the form of their announcement. There is a parallel case where the praetor omitted modifying the language of his counsellors.

Cicero quotes an edict in which the praetor sets out the exact rights of plaintiffs authorized to take provisional possession of the property of defendants because the latter obstruct the progress of a lawsuit.[4] The edict begins by saying that 'it appears proper for them to be in possession in the following manner',

---

[1] The late composition of the Origins is confirmed by Cicero, Sen. 11. 38, to be discussed presently, and Pliny, Hist. Nat. 3. 14. 114.   [2] Sen. 11. 38.
[3] 2. 3. 85. 419. See, e.g. Cuq, *Manuel*, 2nd ed., 1928, 468.   [4] Lenel, 423.

eos ita videtur in possessione esse oportere. This is most strange. For one thing, nowhere else does the praetor issue a general ordinance by means of 'it appears'. He speaks his mind very directly: 'I shall do so and so', 'People should do so and so'. For another thing, as we have seen,[1] nowhere else does he refer to his own regulations as what is 'proper', as *oportere*. The term is reserved for the civil law. I am not implying that the jurists commenting on the Edict may not write, say, *aequissimum praetori visum est legatarium cavere*, 'it appeared to the praetor very equitable that a legatee should give security',[2] or *legatorum nomine satisdari oportere praetor putavit*, 'the praetor considered it proper that security should be given for legacies'.[3] But in the Edict the terms are not applied in this fashion.

To be sure, having enumerated a long series of grounds on which he will grant *restitutio*, the praetor adds:[4] 'similarly if any other just ground will appear to me to exist', *item si alia mihi iusta causa esse videbitur*. This, however, is an entirely different use of the verb. It denotes here a future decision by the praetor about a specific case to be brought before him; it does not denote a rule. The same is true of *videbitur* in several other titles;[5] and equally of *videretur* in the senatusconsult of 161 B.C.,[6] which directed the praetor to see to it, in the way that 'would appear' to be best, that no philosopher should stay at Rome. *Videbitur* in the edicts *De his qui deiecerint*[7] and *De sepulchro violato*[8] also refers to a specific future decision, namely, by the judge. The use in the regulation concerning *missio in possessionem* is definitely unique in the Edict.

Incidentally, this is a clear instance of *oportere* denoting not only what you must do but also what you are entitled to do.[9] One of the clauses of the edict defining 'the correct thing' expressly says that the plaintiffs 'are allowed', *licebit*, to perform certain acts. 'The correct thing' covers their privileges as well as their duties and limitations.

---

[1] See above, pp. 15 ff.
[2] D. 7. 9. 1 pr.
[3] D. 36. 3. 1 pr.
[4] Lenel, 120 f.
[5] In *De dolo malo* (Lenel, 114), *De sepulchro violato* (228, in the passage *cuius iustissima causa esse videbitur*), *De inspiciendo ventre* at the end (313), *De damno infecto* (372), and *Si pupillus heres erit* (419).
[6] Bruns, 170.
[7] Lenel, 173.
[8] 228, in the passage *quanti aequum videbitur*.
[9] Cp. above, pp. 10, 12 ff.

The next two provisions are normal. As far as possible, the plaintiffs 'should guard' the property on the spot, *custodiant*, but what cannot be so guarded 'they will be allowed' to take away, *licebit*.

Then there comes another surprise: *dominum detrudere non placet*, 'it is my opinion that one should not eject the owner of the property'. *Placet* occurs in no praetorian edict but this. We should have expected *dominum ne detrudant*, 'they may not eject the owner', *dominus ne detrudatur*, 'he may not be ejected', *dominum detrudere non licebit*, 'they will not be allowed to eject him'—any of these, but not *dominum detrudere non placet*.

Several explanations may be given. But whichever we choose, we shall find that the form goes back to a province other than the praetor's office; and that it was left intact when the praetor adopted material from that province.

One possibility—a remote one—is that the praetor was under the spell of some senatusconsult. In a senatusconsult, which merely informs the magistrate of the senate's view about a situation and the measures that seem to be called for, *videtur* and *placet* are perfectly in order; and the description of the conduct outlined as 'proper', *oportere*, may have meant that only in this way would the plaintiffs remain within the framework of established law and custom. On this assumption, the praetor stuck to the form of a senatusconsult, the form of advice, even while translating advice into practice, into actual rules to be obeyed by the people.

However, it is extremely unlikely that the senate ever dealt with this matter of provisional possession. One might think of the censors who, since they, too, had the task of stating their opinion about affairs under their control, used in their edicts forms similar to those of the senate.[1] But though they might punish an individual creditor who proceeded too harshly against his debtor, they would be even less interested than the senate in a general regulation of these questions.

A somewhat more probable source is arbitration. The senate,

---

[1] Gellius 15. 11. 2.

in a senatusconsult, propounds its view concerning a situation and the best way to deal with it. That is exactly what an arbitrator does in his verdict. Consequently, he also may put *videtur*, 'it appears', or *placet*, 'it is my opinion'. Again, as he normally bases himself on recognized law and practice, a reference to *oportere*, 'the proper thing', is quite natural; and, needless to add, a subjunctive like *custodiant*, 'they should guard', or a phrase like *licebit*, 'they will be allowed', is also in keeping with the style of such a decision.

A good example from public law is the settlement of a dispute between Genoa and its dependencies,[1] where highly detailed problems of possession and use were involved. Here are some paragraphs: 'That land which we judge to be public it appears proper for the inhabitants of the dependencies to possess and use', *castellanos possidere fruique videtur oportere*. 'For this land they should pay Genoa a yearly tax', *vectigal dent*. 'He who possessed land on that date may be allowed to possess and cultivate', *possidere colereque liceat*. That the decision contains future imperatives as well is not surprising. After all, it was the task of the arbitrators to declare *qua lege agrum possiderent*, 'under what law the parties should possess the land in question'. So we meet with provisions of the type: 'No one shall hinder them from collecting wood from the common pasturage', *ne quis prohibeto quominus sumant*.

It is conceivable that what we have before us in the edict discussed is the form of arbitration. The praetor borrowed his rules from, or at any rate modelled them on, awards setting out the exact rights of the disputants. The form 'it appears' etc. survived the transfer from one milieu to another.

But I much prefer a different solution. Closely related to arbitration, both in function and in form, is the giving of expert opinion, the objective discussion of legal problems. *Videtur* and *placet* are here regularly used as introducing the lawyer's view. It looks as if the praetor got this edict from the legal profession. Whether he asked one of them personally, or whether he found the rules in an existing treatise or *responsum*, makes little differ-

[1] Bruns, 402 f.

ence. In either case the history of the matter would have been as follows:

For some time, the praetor had authorized plaintiffs to take provisional possession of the goods of refractory defendants. One by one, difficult questions had arisen: precisely what did this authorization involve?, how far might the plaintiffs go?, at what point might a defendant make a stand? It was the experts alone who could satisfactorily deal with this complicated position. 'The proper way', they explained—and by *oportere* they understood 'the proper way in view of established law and custom', 'the way in which the plaintiffs would avoid collision with the civil law'—'the proper way appears to be this: some things they should guard on the spot, others they will be allowed to take away; but it is our opinion that the owner may not be ejected'. The praetor accepted this counsel; and he failed to alter the form, though, in the edict, it is quite out of place.

Lenel thinks that the edict must have appeared in Julian's redaction. That is very plausible, but if it did, its form may well have been assimilated to the usual form of edicts. For, as we saw in discussing the prohibition *ne quis fecisse velit*, while forms often last even when transplanted to a different province, there is also a tendency, less conservative, for rarer forms to be swallowed up by the commoner; and it seems to have been very strong in the case of the praetorian Edict. In Julian's redaction, quite likely, *eos videtur esse oportere* had become *ut sint*, and *detrudere non placet* something like *ne detrudant*. This, by the way, remains true whether or not the specific explanation I have given of the extraordinary form of the rules concerning provisional possession is accepted.

There is an implication worth noting, namely, that the uniformity of the edicts in Julian's redaction may to some extent be secondary. We have already found evidence for this in the history of the clause 'if so and so is alleged to have occurred'.[1] So the edict on provisional possession need not always have been the only one showing by its form that it originated in

[1] Above, pp. 31, 36.

expert opinion. Of this edict, we happen to know an early, if not the earliest, text, given by Cicero. If we had many more in the version in which they were first published, *videtur* and *placet*, signs of the consultation by the praetor of a jurist or his treatise, might well turn out far from unique. Similarly, other edicts than *De feris* may once have shown the structure, 'No one should wish to have committed this act'.

7. Assimilation of Forms: Absence of the Copula

I⊤ remains to say a few words about the tendency just mentioned, the desire for uniformity, or the instinct of analogy, or whatever we may call it. As a result of it, where two or three forms do not differ from one another too widely, and where such slight differences as there are between them have lost their practical relevance, one form, the dominant one, will become the only one, everything else being absorbed by it. However apt forms may be to persist outside their original surroundings, and even when the matter has undergone changes, I am sure we have lost a good many that once existed through this process of assimilation. It is fairly obvious in the case of the Edict, but it may be true even of statutes.

Perhaps the following example is in point. At first sight, there appears to be no piece of legislation employing the simple nominal sentence, without the copula *esse*, 'to be'. Yet the nominal sentence was frequent in ancient Latin. To be sure, we must not exaggerate. Contrary to what is said by Hirt,[1] *ager rubricosus* in Cato[2] seems to be a pendent nominative, a heading, rather than a full sentence without copula. Its function is no different from that of the relative clause opening the last sentence of the same paragraph: *quae loca sicca erunt*. In other words, the passage *ager rubricosus ibi lupinum bonum fiet* means, not 'the soil should be reddish; lupine will flourish there', but 'reddish soil, lupine will flourish there', or if we translate less pedantically, 'in reddish soil lupine will flourish'—just as *quae loca sicca erunt ibi triticum serito* means 'in places that are dry plant wheat'.[3] Nevertheless there are numerous unambiguous instances of the nominal sentence.

We remember it best from the area where it always remained

---

[1] *Indogermanische Grammatik*, vol. vii (*Syntax II*), 1937, 23.   [2] R.R. 34. 2.
[3] Cp. below, p. 108, *quod subruptum erit* and so on in the *lex Atinia*.

important, from proverbs and epigrams, such as *Summum ius summa iniuria*, 'Most legalism most injustice', *Varium et mutabile semper femina*, 'Woman—fickle and changeful ever'. English examples are: More haste less speed, No names no pack-drill. Let us note that in some of these sayings, if we supplied a verb, it would have to be, not in the indicative, but in a mood signifying a command, such as imperative or jussive. *Ne quid nimis*, Terence's rendering of μηδὲν ἄγαν, means that nothing 'should be carried' to excess.

It may be useful to ask ourselves why the nominal sentence retained a footing, and even went on extending it, precisely in this field of proverbs and epigrams. The answer, in a general form, is that an utterance gains in force, i.e. it becomes both more arresting and easier to remember, by being confined to the very essence of a thought, anything dispensable being dropped. There is, however, a more specific consideration regarding the absence of a copula, namely, that its absence confers on a statement the character of absolute validity, of timelessness. As is well known, one of the reasons why the nominal sentence gradually disappeared from everyday language was that it is less precise than the sentence with a copula. The copula ties the matter down to a definite period, past, present or future— a highly desirable thing in daily commerce. But it is exactly the thing that might not be wanted where an idea was to be represented as a final, never-changing truth. Hence the nominal sentence prevailed in gnomes or *sententiae*, which purport to enshrine the deepest judgments of the wise.

This analysis is confirmed by the predilection for the nominal sentence displayed by the didactic writers. The Wisdom form is intended to add to the weight and dignity of their teachings. Take this passage from Varro:[1] *Neque eadem loca aestiva et hiberna idonea omnibus ad pascendum*, 'Not the same places suited in summer and winter to the pasturing of all species'. Supposing *sunt* were inserted, this would be a simple, unassuming piece of information. The absence of *sunt* makes it into something rather pretentious, a revelation of profound, invariable knowledge

[1] R.R. 2. 1. 16.

which you can cite, and which you can (and I daresay are intended to) cite even apart from its original context—say, in the wider sense of 'to every thing there is a season'.

However, epigrammatic writing at Rome, though its rudiments go back to a very early period, developed in earnest only under Greek influence, from the third century B.C. It did not, indeed, reach its climax until the silver age. Even then there was less of it than is commonly assumed. It looks, for example, as if certain authors tended to omit *esse* in an accusative and infinitive without any epigrammatic intention. Latte, therefore, is not necessarily right in taking it for granted that Tiberius 'coined the principle *deorum iniuriae dis curae*'.[1] True, Tacitus tells us that Tiberius wrote to the consuls *deorum iniurias dis curae*, 'that the wronging of the gods the gods' concern'; but he also tells us that Tiberius wrote *Cassium solitum*, 'that Cassius (had been) regular in taking part in approved games', and *iusiurandum aestimandum*, 'that an oath (was) to be treated so and so', observations far from aphoristic. Had Tacitus reported Tiberius's view in the form of a direct statement, he might well have put the copula: *deorum iniuriae dis sunt* (or *sint*) *curae*.[2]

At any rate, it is quite possible that, before epigrammatic writing became fashionable, the nominal sentence had one or two different functions. *A priori* one would expect an idea to have been given this form of an absolute, incontrovertible truth above all where it was necessary to defend a position against possible attacks, necessary to silence an antagonist. If so, one wonders whether the form was really never put to use by a lawgiver.

As a matter of fact, two provisions of the XII Tables, as they stand in Cicero, do lack a copula. One excludes aliens from usucapion: *Adversus hostem aeterna auctoritas*,[3] 'Against an alien eternal ownership'. The other prohibits certain funeral customs:

---

[1] *Savigny-Stiftung* 67, 1950, *Rom. Abt.*, 58, on Tacitus, Ann. 1. 73.

[2] Note the comparative rarity of the nominal sentence in the direct quotations occurring in Ann. 2. 38, 2. 71. That C. 4. 1. 2 has no nominal sentence proves nothing.

[3] Bruns, 21. I translate very freely; the true meaning of *auctoritas* is that proposed by Huvelin, *Furtum*, 1915, 283 f.

Ne sumptuosa respersio, ne longae coronae, ne acerrae,[1] 'No costly sprinkling, no long garlands, no censers'.

Modern editors of the XII Tables invariably insert a copula into the former, *aeterna auctoritas esto,* 'ownership shall be eternal'; and they refuse to regard the latter—'No costly sprinkling' etc.— as a literal quotation. Admittedly, in both cases, Cicero may have dropped the copula in order to make his own exposition run more smoothly and rhythmically. But on the whole I find that the habit of thus turning sentences handed down with a copula into maxims without one began after his time. In a large proportion of the better-known instances, the change occurred as late as the Middle Ages. Cicero writes *salus publica suprema lex esto;*[2] the omission of *esto* is medieval. Quintilian writes *bis de eadem re ne sit actio;*[3] *ne bis in idem* is medieval. *Semel heres semper heres,*[4] *fur semper in mora,*[5] or, outside the sphere of law, *sapienti sat,*[6] *de nihilo nihil,*[7] are all medieval abbreviations.

On the other hand, there is evidence of nominal sentences being provided with a copula from long before Cicero down to our day. *Summum ius summa iniuria,* without a copula in Cicero,[8] Columella[9] and Jerome,[10] receives a copula in Terence,[11] in the second century B.C., *ius summum saepe summast malitia,* obviously for the sake of the metre. While Plato writes κοινὰ γὰρ τὰ τῶν φίλων,[12] Cicero hopes *amicorum esse communia omnia.*[13] While Hippocrates says ὁ βίος βραχὺς ἡ δὲ τέχνη μακρή[14] and Seneca *vita brevis ars longa,*[15] Goethe, partly forced by his metre,

---

[1] Bruns, 36 f.   [2] Leg. 3. 3. 8.

[3] I.O. 7. 6. 4; *bis de eadem re agere ne (non) liceat (licet)* in Decl. 266. *De eadem re ne bis agatur* in the *lex Acilia* (Bruns, 67) is a conjecture of Mommsen's, quite possible, but less so than, say, *De rebus ex hac lege iudicatis,* which corresponds more closely to the headings immediately preceding and following, and surely finds strong support in a heading farther on (Bruns, 71): *De rebus ex lege Calpurnia Juniave iudicatis.*

[4] The original, fuller version in D. 28. 5. 89; cp. 4. 4. 7. 10 at the end.

[5] The fuller version in D. 13. 1. 8. 1, 20.

[6] The fuller version in Plautus, Persa 4. 7. 19. 729, and Terence, Phormio 3. 3. 8. 541.

[7] The fuller version in Lucretius 1. 150, 205, 2. 287.

[8] Off. 1. 10. 33.

[9] R.R. 1. 7. 2, *summum ius antiqui summam putabant crucem,* not *putabant esse.*

[10] Ep. 1. 14, *ius summum summa malitia.*   [11] Heautontim. 4. 5. 47. 796.

[12] Phaed. 279 C.   [13] Off. 1. 16. 51.

[14] Aph.   [15] Brev. Vit. 1.

partly in order to give the idea a less proverbial and more spontaneous, conversational appearance, makes Wagner exclaim: *Ach Gott, die Kunst ist lang, und kurz ist unser Leben!*[1] *Varium et mutabile semper femina*[2] is immortal as *La donna è mobile*. Of course, where two languages are concerned, we must consider not only the individual case, but also the facilities each language offers in general. There are, for example, languages with virtually no copula; and the nominal sentence is generally less usual in Latin than in Greek, and less usual in German and Italian than in either.

I incline to take Cicero's quotations from the XII Tables seriously, and to see in them the debris of a form of law which at one time answered a definite purpose, but was gradually eliminated from the sources in favour of the more ordinary pattern. The two provisions in question are both directed against the non-Roman world. An alien cannot usucape, he cannot legally acquire a thing, however long it may have been in his hands, unless he paid the Roman owner for it; and the Etruscan fashion of making a burial an occasion for the display of luxury is not tolerated at Rome. When one imagines how these rules may have come into existence—one day, before a Roman court, some foreigner, by appealing to the Roman institution of usucapion, laid claim to an object which its Roman owner never thought of selling and for which he had never received any value; or one day, a family with Etruscan connexions conducted an elaborate, outlandish funeral—it is easy to see why they might have been framed in an exceptionally terse, domineering, hostile tone. Certainly the insertion of a copula seems to render them very much tamer.

There are indications that the XII Tables denied usucapion to a thief as well as an alien, and, presumably, the same form was employed: *Adversus furem aeterna auctoritas*.[3] True, the posttabular *lex Atinia*, which debars from usucapion both the thief

---

[1] Faust 1, Nacht. In Studierzimmer 2, Mephistopheles says: *Die Zeit ist kurz, die Kunst ist lang*. Here also there is a copula, though, needless to say, the contrast to Wagner's complaint is striking.

[2] Virgil, Aen. 4. 569 f.

[3] Daube, *Cambridge Law Journal* 6, no. 2, 1937, 232.

and any third party who may get hold of the stolen object, contains a copula: *Quod subruptum erit, nisi* (or: *dum non*) *in potestatem eius cui subruptum est revertatur, eius rei aeterna auctoritas esto*,[1] 'Whatever has been stolen, so long as it has not returned into the power of the person from whom it was stolen, ownership of that object shall be eternal'. But *esto* may well be due to assimilation to the more usual style of legislation. As there is a long subordinate clause in this statute, the form must in any case be less compact than that of the original rule of the XII Tables. Again, among the regulations concerning funeral rites, we find very early ones of the perfectly ordinary type. A statute attributed to Numa says: *Vino rogum ne respargito*,[2] 'One shall not sprinkle the pyre with wine'. This, however, is no argument against the occasional use, where a situation seemed to call for it, of the rarer form under discussion.

In any case, there is a sign, independent of the texts I have adduced so far, that Cicero did know of ancient laws consisting of nominal sentences. In his De Legibus, where he imitates the style of ancient laws, he proposes the statute:[3] *Periurii poena divina exitium, humana dedecus*, 'Perjury's punishment from the gods destruction, from men disgrace'. It is interesting that he avails himself of the nominal sentence just for this particularly severe, aggressive decree. It may be mere coincidence, but, even if it is, the form is there. It makes one very sceptical about emendations of those rules of the XII Tables that have come down to us without a copula.

I have deferred a somewhat technical question to which these reflections must give rise: Did the machinery of Roman legislation at all admit of a form other than the future imperative? Or to put it differently: How would a law in the form of a nominal sentence fit into the proceedings employed for the passing of laws? The answer is that there appear to be no insurmountable obstacles.

A *lex* in the strictest sense, a *lex rogata*, is proposed by a

---

[1] Huvelin, op. cit. 287, and Daube, op. cit. 232, n. 43.
[2] Bruns, 8.
[3] 2. 9. 22.

magistrate and approved by the popular assembly.[1] The proposal normally shows this structure: *Velitis, iubeatis, ut sit,*
'Would you wish and command that matters should be so and
so', 'that against an alien ownership should be eternal'. That
is to say, the operative part, the actual law, is expressed by
means of *ut* (or *ne*) with the subjunctive. From some texts[2] it
looks as if an accusative and infinitive might also be used. But
ut is more likely to be the genuine thing: it is easier to imagine
writers replacing an *ut*-clause after *velle, iubere* by an accusative
and infinitive than doing the opposite. In any case, it is only
in the subsequent publication that a future imperative is substituted. *Non constat* that it was in no circumstances possible to
substitute a nominal sentence.

We can go even farther. *Non constat* that the proposal itself
never dispensed with the copula. In early Latin, the nominal
sentence seems to have been fairly frequent even in subordinate
clauses. So *velitis iubeatis ut adversus hostem aeterna auctoritas*, without *sit*, is quite conceivable. Terence puts *ne quid nimis* in an
ut-clause:[3] 'For I think the most expedient principle in life is
ut ne quid nimis, that nothing in excess'. We must also consider
that, though in the official proceedings the statute appears first
in the proposal, i.e. in an *ut*-clause dependent on *velitis iubeatis*,
surely, prior to this moment, when a magistrate plans and
composes his law, he does not subordinate it to that phrase.
If we include this unofficial stage, that is, we find that the
independent version stands at the beginning—with a future imperative or a nominal sentence. It is then, for the purpose of
the proposal, brought into grammatical connexion with *velitis
iubeatis*, while the ultimate publication simply restores the
original.

Perhaps the case will become clearer if we contrast it with a
different one. In my first lecture, I mentioned rules saying that
such and such conduct *oportet*, 'was proper'.[4] It is extremely
unlikely that any provision of this kind originated as a *lex*

---

[1] See Mommsen, *Staatsrecht*, vol. iii, pt. 1, 1887, 311 ff.

[2] E.g. Livy 22. 10. 2. Passages like 1. 46. 1 do not really count, since there is
nothing to suggest that the proposal of the law is copied with absolute fidelity.

[3] Andria 1. 1. 34. 61.   [4] See above, pp. 8 ff.

rogata. A proposal 'Would you wish and command that this or that should be proper' makes no sense. You cannot order a thing to be proper; you can only find it so. But that is not what you do when, as lawgiver, you 'wish and command'; it is what you do when, say, as a priest, senator or legal expert you give your opinion as to the right course to take in accordance with established principles. (Hence *oportere* does occur in a *lex rogata* in phrases like 'he shall take steps that all may be done that should properly be done—*quae fieri oporteret*—under this law'.[1] The actual command lies in 'he shall take steps'; the phrase *quae fieri oporteret* describes what will emerge as requisite from an inquiry into the statute. Similarly, *oportere* might be used in titles of sections of a law. They are intended as clues to the contents, not as commands: 'What it is proper to do— *quid fieri oporteat*—in the event of equality of votes'.[2]) Nor is it credible that where a proposal was of the usual type—'Would you wish and command that matters should be so and so', *ut sit*—the term *oportet* was ever introduced into the final publication.

As we have just seen, these difficulties do not exist about the nominal sentence. There is no reason why it should not figure in a proposal, and even where it does not it would be rash to rule out the possibility of the copula being omitted in the subsequent promulgation of the statute.

Two more remarks, and I have done. First, suppose the laws without a copula came into being as *leges datae*, as statutes not arranged between magistrate and people but simply laid down by the former, then the technical problem is even easier. There is no proposal in this case, no 'Would you wish and command' etc. The magistrate dictates, and it is hard to see what should prevent him from using a nominal sentence. (Indeed, in a *lex data*, even *oportet*, the declaration that a certain action is 'proper', may not be absolutely impossible.) Secondly, even if my arguments in favour of the nominal sentence in some early laws

---

[1] Bruns, 71, ll. 73, 80. Cp. above, p. 23.
[2] 149. The *lex Malacitana* is a *lex data*, but this kind of heading would be equally feasible in a *lex rogata*. Cp. above, pp. 51 ff.

should be judged unconvincing—and I admit that they hardly amount to more than a plea that we should keep our minds open on this point—there is little justification for inserting a copula into the provisions from the XII Tables recorded by Cicero. For they might still be old specimens of legal proverbs, legal Wisdom, and lack a copula on this ground, like so many other gnomes. In other words, they might derive, not from any proper legislation, but, for example, from pontifical collections of recognized maxims; and by the time of Cicero, they had come to be regarded, wrongly, as belonging to the primary codification.

If I may borrow from Swift once more, I am glad you have chosen more convenient stations and postures than the young man from Acts who sat in the window and, as Paul was long preaching, sank down with sleep and fell down from the third loft and was taken up dead. He was indeed brought back to life. But—as the Dean put it—however I may exceed St. Paul in the art of setting men to sleep, I do extremely fall short of him in the working of miracles.

PRINTED IN
GREAT BRITAIN
AT THE
UNIVERSITY PRESS
OXFORD
BY
CHARLES BATEY
PRINTER
TO THE
UNIVERSITY